Mystic

"Divine Revelations"

"Celestial Visions" & "Sacred Knowledge"

Rosaline Temple

To Pearl,
Best Wishes
Rosaline Temple
x

MYSTIC

"Divine Revelations"

"Celestial Visions & Sacred Knowledge" 2012

Rosaline Temple All Rights Reserved

Light Body Publishing

21 Brodoway Road, Enderby, BC V0E 1V3

Canada

Text by Rosaline Temple

Cover Art © 2012 Copyright Mari Sue Baga

ISBN: 10: 1469938057

ISBN-13: 978-1469938059

"Mystic" - *Rosaline Temple*

"Divine Revelations, Celestial Visions & Sacred Knowledge"

Light Body Publishing

"Divine Revelations, Celestial Visions & Sacred Knowledge"

for Helene

"Mystic" - *Rosaline Temple*

"Divine Revelations, Celestial Visions & Sacred Knowledge"

Acknowledgment

I would like to take this opportunity to thank my family and friends, all of the people who have assisted me through this incredible mystical journey:

My mother, who brought me into this world and has guided me throughout my life with all of her wisdom and knowledge, and who made it possible for me to travel to so many places; my father who loved and believed in me, and who still comes to visit me in my "dreamtime"; my husband who has been the greatest teacher in my life, and probably other lifetimes! - who continues to love and support me on my path (even though he thinks I am a little "woo woo"); my children, who have constantly encouraged me to document my experiences and have come to understand that their mother was a little "different"; to my sisters who have never doubted me for a minute about the dreams and visions; Helene Dawson, my niece and "Sister of the Rose" who was killed in a tragic car accident a few years before this was published, and who first put me onto this path;

To my friends that I have met since I began this journey who encouraged me to get the work published, I thank each of you: Valerie Glays, my dear friend who became my teacher; Kamal Gill, Dawn Muncaster, and Susan Kulasa, – who encouraged me to document all of the experiences; Magi Pym, who, at a time when I was concerned about not having "credibility" reminded me that I had "direct knowledge"; Rachel Owa, my dear friend, and (I'm quite sure) "sister from a past life"whose words of wisdom gave me that last little push I needed to get this manuscript published! "that according to Kaballah, the definition of SIN is "someone who is given the gift of a spiritual experience, and chooses NOT to share it with the world".

Special thanks to my long- time friend Ruth Chura, who has been my personal "cheerleader" helping me to "get on with the writing" these last few years; Heinz Hoetger, who out of the goodness of his heart wrote such a beautiful testimony; and to Sheila Steele, my new friend and "Sister of the Rose" who was kind enough to help with the editing.

I thank the Divine Mother/ Father G-d for blessing me with so many wonderful visions, dreams and experiences. I feel truly blessed."

"Mystic" - *Rosaline Temple*

Introduction

"To all of you who are experiencing this time of "awakening" and are wondering "What in the world is going on?" I would like to share my story with you, hoping that I can explain the changes that are happening during these times. It is my wish to explain all that I have experienced and learned in such a way that it will be interesting, informative and easy to understand.

I had never considered myself to be "spiritual" or "psychic" in any way at all, other than having a few strange coincidences happen in my life, and I had experienced the odd vivid dream, but in 1995, something quite profound happened. I began having the most amazing visions, and dreams, in which I found myself traveling to such exotic places, such as the pyramids of Egypt. As well, I received a "wake-up call" from a beautiful angel named Ariel. I can hardly explain the magnificence of her "being" and the surprise and amazement that I felt. All of these "happenings" felt as if they were very real and I was able to describe them in explicit detail. They were so phenomenal, that they had a huge impact on my life and have truly changed it forever.

Sometimes I would only hear words, other times I was shown the most beautiful people and places. With each new experience, I searched for truth, verifying that all of this was in fact "real". I began recording all of the information along the way. While history was never one of my best subjects, strangely my thirst for knowledge rapidly grew, and it seemed that I couldn't get enough information.

It was as if something inside me broke open, and I was able to connect with "beings" from the other side. It appeared that these beings were trying to teach or tell me something, and with each visit I became completely emerged with what it was they were wanting of me. I was fascinated with who they were and wanted to know what their story was. I began to notice that what I and many others, for that matter, had thought was just a philosophy or mythology, was in fact real, and that there was a tie – a connection between all of the teachings. Through it all, I kept asking them what it was that I was supposed to be doing with all of this information. I discovered that I was being taught a very sacred and ancient teaching known throughout creation as the "Universal Flower Language".

When it came time to choose a title for this book, I was shown in a vision, the word "Mystic". Upon looking up the meaning, I found the following: "Someone who is blessed with the experience of the Divine, a person who has been profoundly touched by an occurrence that allowed them to believe that they were truly in the presence of a heavenly, or celestial being. The sensation is so phenomenal, that it becomes emblazed into their very heart of their soul, and it becomes their passion to share these experiences with the world." I feel that this word, "Mystic" truly expresses my feelings, and what this book is about. I hope that it will inspire you to pay attention to your dreams, find your passion, and fulfill your "sacred contract"."

"Mystic" - *Rosaline Temple*

PART 1

"Divine Revelations"

"Celestial Visions" & *"Sacred Knowledge"*

"We are in the midst of a great transformation, and many of us are now able to open our hearts and minds to a much higher level. As the world enters this long awaited Age of Aquarius, the new energies surround us, expanding our awareness while challenging our intellectual thoughts about ourselves and other "beings" living on the planet. The more "open" we are, the more aware we become of the many signs around us, and the synchronicities that notably begin manifesting in our lives. Our psychic abilities become stronger, and we may experience vivid dreams or visions, or something quite "unexplainable" causing us to search for answers. We are "awakening" and becoming more aware. Many are beginning to understand that each of us have a "sacred contract" to fulfill, and that we are part of a much greater and higher consciousness."

.........Rosaline Temple

"Mystic" - *Rosaline Temple*

Chapter 1

"A Late-Summer's Night Dream"

Disenchanted, I stood mesmerized as I gazed out the window and watched the leaves falling to the ground. It was late August, 1987, and I could still smell the freshly-mown grass, yet already the Autumn leaves were beginning to change their colour. I couldn't help but notice how they looked like the pieces of a giant puzzle waiting to be assembled into a huge crimson coloured blanket. I wondered if this was a representation of my own life. Fragmented bits, lost pieces - would I ever be able to put the pieces back together? Would I be able to weave my life into the vibrant tapestry that I had always imagined it would be?

As usual, nothing life-changing had happened that day. As a matter of fact everything seemed quite the same as it always did. Painting one minute, chasing after the kids the next - dreading calls from collection agencies, and wondering which husband would walk through the door - Dr. Jekyll or Mr. Hyde. No strange occurrences or events surfaced on that day to warrant anything special or unusual.

I could feel the tears welling up. Blinking several times, I tried to control the overwhelming emotions that were coming over me. Unsuccessful, they quickly avalanched spilling down my cheeks, and I began wiping away my tears. "Is this it? "Is this all there is?" I thought. "Surely there must be more to life than this."

As I crawled into bed that night, I could feel the walls of despair, and confusion closing in on me. Even though we had our "ups and downs," I loved my husband and children with a passion, but I couldn't help but wonder why the chains of motherhood seemed so confining. I choked back the sobs, and could feel the tears streaming onto the pillow. I silently waited, longing for sleep to engulf me, allowing me to escape to another place and time. I drifted off to my "magical" time, my place of rejuvenation.

I had an amazing ability, during those years, to submerge myself into the deepest of sleeps, where nothing would disturb me. But this particular night was quite different, because sometime after the darkest hours of midnight, at the very quietest time - I was gently awakened. The only way that I can describe it, is to say that there appeared to be a "being of pure light" standing right next to the bed, watching over me. A soft blue glow shimmered from this long-robed figure, and the most angelic yet protective feelings emanated from this masculine essence. Strangely enough, I wasn't frightened at all. In fact, the strongest sensation of "knowingness" come over me. It was as if I had been expecting him, and had long awaited his arrival.

Ever so gently, his hand reached out towards me. I wasn't quite sure what it was he seemed to be offering - a "gift" of sorts. I didn't hesitate to reach out to receive it, as if I had an unconscious recognition of what he was offering. This "angelic like" being placed something in my open palm, and as I held this radiant object, I gazed upon it, wondering what it might be. I thought it looked quite simply like an orange, except that it was glowing and appeared to be made of pure light. Hypnotically, this crystal-like sphere began to develop petals, like those you would see on a delicate flower. And, as they opened - this luminescent orange magically transformed itself into a beautiful lotus blossom. I immediately felt as if I was floating above my body, and the most wonderful sensation came over me. Words couldn't possibly describe what I was feeling! I knew I had a huge smile on my face, and I was sure I must have looked like a "Cheshire Cat" with this silly grin - and at the same time, I kept wishing and hoping this feeling would last forever. The thought raced through my mind. "This must be what heaven is like, and if this is it - I'm staying! "

Seconds later, like a bird falling from the sky with a thud, I found myself back in my body. I immediately noticed how heavy I felt, and I seemed to have acquired a lot of aches and pains I previously hadn't been aware of, but of course I had also never been "out of my body" before either - and that experience was phenomenal! I was ecstatic. I could hardly believe how amazing I had felt.

The next morning I kept thinking about what had happened to me. I was completely shocked and truly astonished that anything like this could possibly happen, and I wanted to share it with the whole world!

I was working as an artist at the time, teaching oil painting to adults from my home. I could hardly wait for everyone to arrive that day. I was excited to tell everyone about "my experience" and to see their reaction. When they arrived, I immediately blurted out my story, describing every last detail - thinking that everyone would find it as fascinating as I did, but the response that I got was not quite what I had expected. While most people thought it was incredible and considered me to be "lucky" some of the others felt quite differently One of the older women automatically categorized it as a "religious" experience! I was amused at this, considering that I wasn't religious at all. Not that I haven't always believed in a "higher power" or God, but I certainly wouldn't consider myself to be "religious", or even "righteous" for that matter. Besides what did "religion" have to do with it anyway?

Another response really surprised me. She was a woman in her late twenties, who considered herself to be a "born again Christian". For some strange reason, which I still don't understand to this day, she believed that in order for me to have had this type of an experience, I would have had to be practicing some kind of "black magic" and that I must surely be a witch! This really confused me. How could something so incredibly positive be seen in such a negative way? I had considered this to be one of the most amazing and beautiful experiences of my life! What ever would make her think it could be bad? After all, it wasn't something that I had "conjured" up! It was just something that happened.

I learned very quickly that my experience, wasn't meant to be shared with just anyone, and so I filed it into the recesses of my mind. It wasn't until another eight years had passed, that I thought about it once more.

Chapter 2

"An Industrial Revolution"

It was the Summer of 1995 - and definitely my favorite season of year. The Leo in me was purring, looking forward to escaping and disconnecting from the electronic devices, which had seemed to take over my life as a realtor. My mom came to the rescue. She seemed to have an uncanny way of asking me to "do her a favor" which quite amazingly would turn into a "mini get-away" for me. This time she was going back east for a visit, and asked me to drive her from Vancouver, BC to Sea-Tac Airport in Washington, where she would be catching her flight. (We discovered a long time ago, that flying via US Airlines was a lot less expensive than flying Canadian!) The timing was perfect, because I could scoot down to pick up my daughter Melissa who was visiting some relatives in Tacoma, plus I would get to spend some quality time with both my mother and daughter - a rare commodity.

My mother and I left Vancouver Sunday afternoon, having made the decision to stay in a motel overnight. Mom, a cute little bottle-dyed redhead, made sure that I caught up on all the latest family gossip (as I'm sure most mothers do) as we drove along the I-5, and I enjoyed her company for the two hours it took to get there. In Seattle, we found lodging close to the airport, checked in, and then went out for dinner.

The following morning everything went smoothly. We got up early, and I helped my mom get her overnight bag packed. Then I went downstairs to help her get safely onto the shuttle bus that would take her to the airport. After seeing her off, I grabbed a coffee for my morning "java fix" and then went back to our room to get myself ready. As I began collecting my things, I turned on the television to catch the traffic report and the early morning news, and was caught off-guard. The news anchor was reporting that all the airports were being carefully searched and watched. Apparently, a threatening letter had been sent by the "Unibomber" stating that a bomb had been placed somewhere inside one of the airports. The Unibomber was an infamous American "recluse" who had been sending mail bombs to airports and other places, beginning in 1978. Knowing that my mother had just left for Sea-Tac airport, I could feel terror flood through my veins. What could I possibly do? The bus had already left and I knew that she would already be somewhere inside the airport. The threats appeared to be focused around LAX, so I tried to calm myself down, thinking that she would be ok as she was traveling east, not south, and G-d willing, she would be fine. I finished my coffee, grabbed my bags, and in a state of panic, left for my niece's place in Tacoma. It was gorgeous out – definitely convertible weather, but unfortunately, I wasn't driving one! The sun was shining, there was hardly any traffic, and it surely didn't seem right to have such an awful threat taking place on such a beautiful day. Normally, I would have had the music blaring, but on that day I listened to the news, trying to keep informed about the Unibomber. As I traveled along the I-5, I couldn't help but wonder why some people have the audacity to do such terrible things, and I kept thinking about what a horrific place this world had become! I remember thinking to myself "If G-d exists, then why does he allow all of this evil to happen?" It was as if the world was becoming ever so more violent. I felt angry, and I was questioning God. Eventually, I turned off the radio, and put on some tapes, trying not to think anymore about the threat. As I got closer to Tacoma, I happened to take the wrong exit ramp and found myself crossing a bridge, ending up in an area that was unfamiliar, very unattractive, and very industrial. I realized that I had made a mistake, and turned around, making sure I was heading in the right direction, this time. As I write this, I realize that it was almost metaphoric for my life.

I began thinking about my niece, Helene, and her family, wondering how they were coping. Her father, Chuck had died quite unexpectedly, almost a year prior, which had devastated the family. Helene had moved her whole family into her mother's home right after her father had passed away, to help ease the pain of the "loss" for her mother.

I finally arrived around 6:00 am. They lived in a modest white cottage-style home, with a large veranda that ran the width of the house. As I went up the stairs, I thought about my brother-in-law Chuck, knowing it would seem strange not to see him there. It was still quite early, but the door had been left unlocked for me, so I let myself in. Everyone was still asleep. My sister-in-law Natalie had pre-set the coffee-maker for me the night before, and the aroma met me as I opened the door. I thought about what my poor sister-in-law had been through, and my heart went out to her.

As I helped myself to my second cup that morning, I went into the living room, to turn on the TV for a news update on the Unibomber. I was relieved to learn that no bombs had gone off, and they were announcing that it was a false alarm.

I began switching channels, looking for something else to watch, but they all appeared to be talking about the Unibomber. I was astonished to discover that he was considered to be highly intellectual – a child prodigy who went to Harvard, and eventually worked at as an Asst. Professor at Berkeley. His real name was Dr. Theodore John Kaczynski. I found it hard to believe that this highly intelligent person would behave in such a manner, and I couldn't help but wonder why.

As the discussion went on, I learned that he opted out of society in 1971, moving to a cabin in the woods. As the area around him became more and more destroyed by "development" he became very angry and began sending out mail bombs to several universities and airports. He had sent a letter to a newspaper, stating that he would stop the bombings if they would publish his manuscript. There was a lot of controversy about whether or not it should be published, which was what the TV show was about.

I thought it odd that while driving to Tacoma, I had taken a wrong turn, ending up in an industrial area, which I found distasteful. It was as if I was being shown on the physical level, why the Unibomber was so angry.

I recalled the time when I had just returned from Mexico, only to find that the beautiful row of sixty foot trees along the back of our property had been cut down. All of the houses on the street behind had been torn down, burned to the ground, to make room for townhouses. It didn't bother me that the homes had been removed, but there really was no reason for the trees to be cut, and I was truly enraged. I can honestly say that I felt "invaded" and almost as if I had been raped. It was the first time that I realized how much I loved and felt connected to nature.

After learning more about this man, I was able to understand his fury, although I didn't agree with his "terrorist" antics. He had already killed three people, and injured twenty-three others, which to me was unacceptable, frightening, and evil. In the meantime, I was relieved that no bombs had been found, and that my mother would arrive in an airport that was bomb-free.

Even though I understood why the Unibomber was doing this, I couldn't help but question God, wondering why he would allow these types of things to happen, and why our world seemed to have become so full of violence. I was feeling saddened, disgusted and disillusioned. I turned off the television.

Chapter 3

"A Message From My Father"

I glanced around the room, and could see many photos and other items that reminded me of my brother-in-law Chuck. He was a very large man, with a personality to match. It was hard to believe that he was gone, and I definitely felt the void. As I sat there, sunk into his well-used couch, I couldn't help but think about him. Then I noticed that there were a lot of books and tapes lying on the coffee table, all of which had the same subject matter - "life after death" and "near death experiences". I remembered that my niece Helene had been saying that she thought that her father was trying to contact them shortly after he died. Chuck used to like playing tricks on his kids, especially Helene, so I wasn't surprised when she said that many unusual things had been happening. She said "objects would fall for no reason, and electrical appliances like their fridge, microwave, VCR and television started going on the blink". She even felt him grabbing her finger or touching her – that would be Chuck! The whole family had sensed his presence, and so they began reading and watching everything they could find about "life after death".

I began thinking about my own experiences shortly after my father had passed away. I also used to sense his presence, and while I loved my father very much, at times I became a little frightened. I can remember thinking "Okay, Dad, I know you're here, but please don't show yourself to me!" I don't know what I would have done if I had actually seen him!

About a month after my father had died, the most interesting thing occurred. It was Spring, 1978. I had just dropped off my son at his Kindergarten class in the early morning, and while driving home I began listening to a talk show on the radio called "The Gary Bannerman Show"- a very popular program at the time. Gary's guest that morning, was a well-known psychic, and many people were calling in to speak with him. They kept announcing that he would be leaving immediately after the show because he had a flight to England, which he had to catch. I became quite intrigued with the program, as he apparently seemed to be able to contact people who were "on the other side".

When I got home, I quickly turned on the stereo in the living room, and sat down to catch the balance of the program. Most of the people calling in were hoping to contact a relative or friend who had died. I remember wondering if I should call in, thinking to myself "maybe I could get in touch with my dad."

Just then something quite amazing happened! The psychic was addressing a caller saying *"You had someone close to you pass* away recently, didn't you? About a month ago!" The woman replied "*No, I haven't*". Then he said "*Does the name "Mary" mean anything to you?*" The woman said "*no*". He continued "*This is coming in very strongly.... Does the family name "Berman" mean anything to you?*" Again she said "*no*". He began asking everyone else waiting to speak to him if this information pertained to them. They all said "*no*".

"*What happened to your engagement ring?*" he went on. The woman replied that she had no engagement ring and that she had never been engaged. "*Not your engagement ring, but your mother's engagement ring! Not a fancy engagement ring, but a nice one.*" The way he said it gave me goosebumps, as his voice reminded me of how *exactly* my father would have spoken. An eerie feeling swept through me. "*He had given it to you as a gift, but you don't have it anymore*" he went on to say, and wanted to know where it was!"

At that point, I began to think how weird and coincidental it was that he was saying those things, because my first name is Mary, and dad had given me my mother's engagement ring a few months before he died. I didn't have it anymore because all of my jewelry had been stolen when our house had been broken into". As for the family name "Berman" mentioned on the radio show, I just couldn't make any sense out it.

At that very moment the telephone rang. It was my mother. She knew that I had been at an art auction the night before and that my

14

sister-in-law had bought me a painting. My mother wanted to know who the artist was. I looked at the painting, and saw that the name was *Sari Berman*. I could feel the hair standing up on my skin! I ran back to the phone, told my mother the name of the artist, and asked her if that name "Berman" should mean anything to me. She told me that the name Berman was actually my father's mother's maiden name. (My father's side of the family had died when I was very young, and strangely, I had never known my great grandparents' name.) I became very excited, and immediately told my mother about the psychic on the talk show, and all the 'coincidences'. We both agreed that the messages definitely seemed to be directed at me, and that I should call the radio station right away.

Well I called and called, but by the time I got through, the psychic had already left the building. I knew they had announced previously that he would be leaving for England right after the show, but I had thought that there was a slight chance that I would catch him. The woman who answered the phone began questioning me as to why I was calling now. I explained to her that everything he had been saying to one of the callers, actually pertained to me. She told me that he kept mentioning *Edinburgh, Scotland* – asking me if it meant anything to me, as it apparently was quite important. I had missed part of the show while I was talking to my mother, so I hadn't heard mention of it. I said that Edinburgh didn't mean anything at all to me, and that I had never been to Scotland, nor had I any relatives from there (that I was aware of) but explained to her that everything else he had said seemed to apply to me!

She kept asking me if I had been trying to call in, or if I had been waiting on the line to speak with him. I said "no" and went on to explain that I had just been sitting in my living room listening to the show, but had *thought* that I should call in. She was quite surprised that this could happen, and of course, so was I. I thought that maybe there was a message for me, although I wasn't quite sure what it was. There was mention of a ring, and the name of the artist on the painting was the same as my grandmother's maiden name.

Was my father trying to tell me to begin painting again? I had attended art college when I was much younger, but after getting married and having children, I never seemed to have the time to do anything for myself anymore. I had been wanting to take oil painting lessons for several years, and had approached many artists in the malls, but I hadn't been able to find anyone that was willing to teach. But, quite amazingly, within days after receiving the "message" on the radio, I walked into a shopping plaza, and couldn't help but notice a display of paintings with a sign saying "If you're interested in oil painting lessons, inquire inside". Suddenly my wish was being fulfilled. I quickly went inside to get more information. I was able to get in touch with the artist, and I immediately signed up for ten lessons. At the time, I had wondered if my father had done some "arranging" from the other side, as it seemed so coincidental.

Being able to paint once again was very fulfilling for me, as I was finally able to express my creative side, and I was enjoying it immensely. Even my friends were surprised at how quickly I caught on, and some of them even commissioned me to do some work for them. When I first began taking my lessons, I had mentioned to my teacher, Dave Preston, that I would like to learn how to teach, but had no idea that my career as an instructor would begin so quickly. Within weeks, Dave realized that he needed an assistant, and began training me. It was not too long after that I began teaching my own classes, but unfortunately, Dave began severely suffering from arthritis, and decided to move back to Alberta. The weather in British Columbia was far too damp for Dave, causing him a lot of pain. As my husband had a truck, he helped Dave move his family back to Edmonton. As it turned out, there wasn't enough room for a lot of the easels and other studio items, so he left them for me and we stored them in our barn. My students were really upset that the studio was closing, as they wanted to continue with their lessons. In fact, they were so determined about it, that several of them donated space in their homes for me to use. At first I thought it would be until they finished their ten lessons, but each week, one of them would bring somebody new. Eventually, through my students' persistence, I was convinced to open my own art studio - and I had all the easels and paraphernalia to do so.

As I thought about my father's death, and the synchronicity of hearing the "message" over the radio, I thought about the "ring" that had been mentioned, once again. My father, prior to his passing, had given me some gold hoop earrings. Unfortunately, a few years later, I lost one, so my mother suggested that I have the other one made into a ring, and took it to her jeweler to see what he could do with it. After looking at it, he suggested that I might want to have a few stones put on the ring. My mother asked if he would take a painting in return, to which he agreed.

Enthusiastically I went to work creating a painting, entitled "The Diamond Cutter" for his office, and personally delivered it to him. It turned out that the Jeweler was an art lover, and after receiving the painting, he felt that the diamonds weren't enough, and he added a beautiful emerald onto the ring. I was thrilled! He then informed me that he would like me to have a show of my work, stating that he would arrange and pay for everything, including the framing. There was only one stipulation - he wanted all the paintings to be based on the stories of the Old Testament. I didn't know too much about my Judaic roots, as I wasn't religious, but I realized that this was a wonderful opportunity, so of course I agreed to do it. As it turned out, I found some of the information quite interesting, and eventually it turned out to be quite valuable.

After thinking about the psychic on the radio show, I have come to believe that "the message from my father" had been his way of telling me to start painting again, and that it would be a way for him to give me another ring!

Eventually I had the opportunity to meet the psychic from the talk show. I had to book an appointment three months in advance, and I was really excited about meeting with him. Since I had received a "message" without him even talking to me, I believed and hoped that he would have something quite incredible to tell me, in person. I was especially hoping to discover some information about Edinburgh, Scotland. When we finally met, I explained to him what had happened previously over the air. I was surprised, when he claimed that it was absolutely impossible, and that the message couldn't possibly have been meant for me! It seemed strange to me, that he acknowledged "contact with the *spiritual world*" but couldn't believe that the information given, could pertain to anyone other than those that were calling in. He had nothing extraordinary to tell me. It showed me that people who are psychic, may get very clear messages some of the time, but not all of the time. Although he tried his best, I have to say that it was a huge disappointment for me, but I knew with all my heart, that the message had been from my father, as there were just too many coincidences. I left there still wondering about Edinburgh, Scotland and what my connection was to it.

Chapter 4

"Angels & Oranges"

My train of thought was suddenly broken as Helene came into the living room. I explained to her that I was totally intrigued by the books that she had lying around, and had been thinking about my own experiences surrounding my father's death. I listened to her as she shared her personal experiences and feelings about her own father's passing. Then she began telling me about some of the books that she had been reading, and also about a television show she had enjoyed watching called "The Other Side". Helene had taped almost all of the series. I watched a few of them, which I found very interesting, and she loaned me a couple of books to take home and read.

I read the first book while I was still there. It was called "Embraced by the Light" by Betty Jane Eadie, which had quite an effect on me. It was about a woman who had a "near death experience" (sometimes referred to as a NDE) that had lasted for several minutes, much longer than most. Her memories of heaven were phenomenally descriptive, and included so much information, that it was quite devastating (to say the least) and quite literally almost made you "want to die" just to experience it! She explains that she had learned many things, during her brief time there. One of the things she mentioned, was that "each of us has a special mission in life" and that "everyone we see or pass by is supposed to trigger some kind of memory within us" to remind us of our purpose. Apparently, it doesn't matter who we are or what we do, even if we are just a bum on the street, that person's mission may be to remind one specific person to give to the poor. I thought about the Unibomber, guessing that he believed his mission was to bring awareness to the devastation that industrialization was causing to the earth. I wondered what G-d would think of his "method of awareness". And, of course, I couldn't help but wonder what my personal "mission" was supposed to be.

My daughter and I left for home the following morning. As I drove along the highway back towards British Columbia I thought about the book, and also the videos I had watched. I recalled that many of the people that shared their experiences spoke about a wonderful feeling of "love and light". I realized that the feeling they were talking about, was similar to the experience I had in 1987 with the angelic "being of light" and the orange that turned into a lotus blossom.

One of the other amazing things I had discovered while watching the videos, was that many of the guests on the show had profound gifts. Some were very psychic and others had gifts of healing. Some of them could actually take people's pain away by laying their hands on them. I had never known or even heard of such a thing, and was in awe that anyone could possibly do this. I was very intrigued and wanted to know how they could accomplish such an amazing feat. I decided to do some more research on the subject, and of course wondered if I would ever be able do anything like that.

I began reading the books that Helene had given me, and I seemed to have this incredible thirst for knowledge. I knew of a metaphysical bookstore in our area and decided to pay them a visit. I looked around the store specifically for some books that might teach me how to do "hands on" healing, and was able to find a couple that looked interesting. I was just about to pay for them, when I noticed a sign on one of the tables that said "newly released". I felt compelled to take one "last look" before paying for the ones I had already stacked on the counter. As I scanned the table, I suddenly noticed one particular book, and could hardly believe my eyes! Directly in front of me, was a book called "Angels and Oranges". I was awestruck! The cover of the book had a painting created by an artist by the name of Phyllis Serota. It was a bowl of oranges set on a table, surrounded with people, with angels flying above them. I had never come across any books or material that related to "oranges & angels" together, but when I saw it, my memory was immediately flooded with the experience I had so many years prior. Of course, my visitor wasn't a winged angel, but a "being of pure golden light" but that didn't matter to me as I felt that my visitor carried the same angelic-like essence, and I certainly felt that finding this book, was much more than coincidental. I never looked inside, so I had no idea what the book was about, but I immediately knew that I had been led to this specific piece of work, and that it was something that I needed to read. I brought it home, and discovered it to be one of the most beautiful pieces of literature I had ever come across. It was just filled with messages of love.

The author of the book, Erin Caldwell, stated that she was just an ordinary woman, leading an ordinary life, when she suddenly had the overwhelming feeling that she had to sit down and write. In fact she felt that if she didn't express herself, she would burst! As she began to put pen to paper, the most beautiful poetic messages came pouring out. She stated that she began receiving the messages sometime in 1987 or 1988. This was strangely coincidental, because that was around the same time that I had the visit from my "Being of Light". I kept reading the "Angels and Oranges" book over and over, discovering that I just couldn't put it down. It was about a week or two later that I began having the most incredible dreams and visions as I fell asleep each night. Although I think that the dreams were more involved, I was only able to remember small parts.

The first vision I had was a beautiful violet -colored door, made of crystal or glass. It was majestic, and appeared to be made of large squares of "amethyst". It was framed in a wide band of gold that was embossed with raised lettering or intricate design. It was extremely elegant, and it gave me the impression that it led to a very important place. I can't recall if I went through the door or not, but I remember seeing it very well. The following evening there were thousands of baby angels, flying in the same direction, blowing little horns and trumpets. My heart felt excited at the appearance of these cherubim, and I felt that I needed to share these experiences with the world.

I had never written to an author before, but at the back of the book I noticed there was a telephone number and address. It turned out that the book had been written right here in British Columbia, on Saltspring Island and I noticed that the publisher had a note asking for comments. I called the number and spoke to the publisher telling her about my experience with the "Being of Light and the Orange" and especially about the visions I was experiencing while reading the book. She asked that I fax her a letter explaining, in detail, what had occurred. She also informed me that many people were contacting her, telling her that they too felt that the book had been written especially for them. I had read a few metaphysical books in the past, but nowhere had I ever read or seen anything relating to angels or "beings of light" and oranges. I looked at the book I had just brought, and noticed that it had been published in June of 1995, only one month prior. I suddenly had this inner "knowingness" that I wasn't supposed to come across this information until this time.

I began to notice that everything that was happening in my day-to-day life was interacting with my visions and dreams. There seemed to be a lot of synchronicities, and as I shared them with my friends and relatives, everyone kept emphasizing that I needed to keep track of all of these experiences so that I wouldn't forget them. And so I did!

July 13th, 1995. I was expecting my mother to return from her trip. I dreamt that she called to say that they were going to be late because of a bad storm and that they had to close down the airport. I woke up thinking "What a funny thing to dream, a snowstorm in July!" Our weather was beautiful, and so was the weather in Seattle. But sure enough, the phone rang shortly after, and it was my mother calling from Toronto. "You wouldn't believe the weather we're having here! We've been experiencing lightening storms and they've had to close down the airport!" When I had first woken up from the dream; I seemed to think that the message was about Sea-Tac Airport, where I had originally dropped off my mother. But of course, she was leaving from Toronto, and although she had communicated to me in the dream that they were experiencing a "storm" - I had *assumed* it was snow storm, not lightning. In any case, I definitely received the message!

I began wondering if I was becoming psychic. Well I guess I was, but in quite a different way. I seemed to be receiving all of the messages and images in my sleep through my dreams, and sometimes I had the distinct feeling that I was woken up in the middle of the night and given information. I was also beginning to be shown a lot of hieroglyphics and symbols, which strangely enough were Egyptian. As I come from a Judaic background, I had been taught that our ancestors had been slaves in Egypt. For as long as I can remember, we celebrated our freedom every year at Passover, which has been done for centuries, ever since Moses led his people out of that country. So even though I find their artwork fascinating, it seemed really odd to me that I would be dreaming about Egypt.

The "Angels and Oranges" book didn't seem to be based on anything Egyptian; so I was still at a loss as to why this was happening to me. My mother and I *had* been to Las Vegas in February, and we had visited The Luxor Hotel, which looks exactly like a Pyramid. Was it possible that this was why I was having these experiences? I remember being completely mesmerized and fascinated with the Egyptian jewelry and everything else they had on display. In fact, I could have spent the entire day there, but I had to leave as I had pre-arranged a time to meet my mother and her friends who were waiting for me, and I was already late. Was it possible that my enchantment with the Egyptian artifacts set off the dreams? I couldn't help but wonder if this was happening to anyone else who had visited the Luxor. I had originally meant to visit the King Tut exhibit that was on display there, but somehow got in the wrong line-up. I ended up watching a small virtual reality movie, which gave you the impression that you were flying around inside a pyramid, which didn't make a bit of sense to me. Little did I know....

Chapter 5

"Signs of Egypt"

Egyptian hieroglyphics, began streaming into the area of my forehead known as the "third eye". They were a beautiful shimmering gold and moved in such a way that one would think they had a life of their own, and then the signs and symbols appeared. Many of them I was unfamiliar with, but began searching for information on each one.

The first symbol that appeared was an "Ankh", a cross with an oval opening at the top, which I learned, was the symbol used by the ancient Egyptians to represent "eternal life". Ankhs are often seen in Egyptian Papyrus works of art, being held in the hands of the Gods and Goddesses. They were often gifts given to Egyptian Royalty, as well as the Priests and Priestesses of ancient times. Eternal life? Was immortality possible? Would one want to live forever? With what was happening on the earth today, this was questionable!

The second sign was a very ornate looking hand, known throughout the Middle East as a "Hamsa". I recognized it immediately when it was shown to me, as I had often seen this symbol while traveling in the Middle East in the early "70's". Everywhere I went, I noticed this charm either hanging in stores, or being worn on people's clothing. It is supposed to represent the "Hand of God" and is used to ward off evil spirits.

The third sign was a fish. The actual drawing had bones inside, and at the time, I thought it really odd that I would be shown a fish. Eventually I was told that this was one of the symbols used for Christianity. After looking into it further, I discovered that this belief actually stemmed from ancient Egyptian times when it was used to represent the Dolphin and "spirituality". Dolphins were highly regarded in ancient times, both in Egypt and Greece, where there were temples built in their honour. I have since learned that this shape is also known as a Vessica Pisces, an ancient mystical symbol used to represent "the divine" merging with matter. Was that possible?

In another dream, I noticed that I was holding an object in the palm of my hand. When I looked at it closer, I realized that it was a small carving of a bird, rectangular in shape, and made of Marble or Alabaster - about two or three inches high and beige in color. I thought it was an Owl or an Eagle, as it looked like a bird with its wings closed and perched. It was kept in a black velvet pouch, and I was given the impression that this was supposedly something *very* meaningful to me. It didn't look familiar to me at all, and it certainly didn't trigger any specific memory in my mind. I knew nothing about it, nor was I able to find any information pertaining to it for the longest time. But I knew from the way they were showing it to me that it was something I *should* have remembered and that it was of significant importance. It was years later that I discovered that this was commonly known in Egypt as "Horus" the Egyptian Sun God, who was depicted as a Hawk.

In 1998, I was telling a friend who had just returned from Egypt about some of my visions, and I mentioned the little statue. I described it to her, asking if she had ever come across any statues of Horus that looked like that, and if so, whether they came in a black velvet pouch. She told me that almost everywhere you go in Egypt you see statues of Horus and lots of "little black velvet pouches!" She said, "They put *everything* in them!" I have to say, that I was glad to get confirmation of what I had seen. She told me that according to the Egyptian teachings, Horus was known as a very understanding and compassionate G-d who protected children, as well as the elderly. That is why the Egyptian symbol known as the "Eye of Horus" is commonly used for protection. Later on I had a vision of an "eye" and even though it sounds strange, I had the distinct feeling that it was also alive. There is a legend that one day Horus will return and bring with him a "Golden Age" which some people believe to be now.

This whole "Egyptian thing" was very interesting to me. It was as if I was being shown different parts of a movie that I needed to re-assemble, in order to see the "big picture". More importantly, I needed to find out why I was being shown these symbols.

Most unusual, was the profile of a Winged Lion. It appeared simply as a line drawing with the words "Five Breeds" or "Five Species" (I can't be sure) typewritten beneath it. I wasn't sure what the words represented, but since that time I have come across many sculptures of Winged Lions. They are often found in front of temples, and the symbol can also be found on the emblems of Royalty, and on religious documentation. I began to see the symbol as a representation of spirituality and royalty, which is interesting, because the "being" they had brought my attention to "Horus" was considered to be not only a god, but also a king. There were also several feminine deities in Egypt that were depicted as humans with lions' heads. One thing for sure, I was beginning to learn quite a bit about the ancient Egyptians and their philosophy.

At other times, several *live* lions appeared to me during my dream state, and I was quite comfortable around them. In fact, I experienced immense love, not fear. In the book called "The Winged Lion of Timbavati" by Linda Tucker, she states that the sun and the lion are directly linked because they are of the same life-force. She states that the shamans say "White Lions" are considered to be "Lions of God" heavenly messengers bringing the laws of the sun to earth. They hold the same vibration as the sun itself, the very essence which first created life on this planet. It seemed quite coincidental that I was being shown these images during the latter part of July, the time of Leo, which was also my personal sun sign. Was there a connection?

My mystical journey continued, and in one of the dreams, I recall finding an object in the palm of my hand. It was a small pillar, with a pyramid at the very tip of it. The object was approximately two inches wide at the bottom and about four inches tall, embossed with foreign writing. Of course, this was an obelisk, which is also found in Egypt! What was unusual about this item was the experience I had with it. I ran my left thumb along the hieroglyphics on the obelisk, and suddenly flew out of my body. It felt as if I was floating.... I was quite shocked that I was able to do this, and wondered where I had learned to do this.

Of course, obelisks come in many sizes, and some are extremely large, chiseled out of granite mines. I learned that in ancient times, they were transported by boat to the many temples along the Nile, where they were erected. Some were massive in size, and nobody knows exactly how they were able to transport them over land and erect them without having them break, as they were many tons in weight.

As the on-going theme of my dreams appeared to be mostly Egyptian, eventually a pyramid was revealed to me. I recall feeling immensely overwhelmed at the sight of it, as it appeared to be quite radiant and intensely stunning, as it was covered in a layer of gold, shining brilliantly in the shimmering sand. I was looking down upon it from above so that the Pyramid was more to the left and the sand came out around it. I seemed to be floating above it. The pyramid also looked as if it had a "landing strip" on the very top of it. Suddenly, an opening in the ground appeared and beneath it was an island. It was very small, and had palm trees on it. To the right of this, appeared another image within the same vision. I could see an entrance to a temple, in front of the doorway was a type of totem pole. It had beautifully carved images of animals stained in rich dark mahogany. The carving was smooth with rounded edges, and had a highly polished finish, quite different than our Native American totems. Although I had never been there, it reminded me of what you might see in Tahiti or some place in the South Pacific.

I got the impression that I was being shown that the Pyramid was also a temple, and that it was somehow connected to the island that I was shown, which I thought might possibly be on the other side of the world. I found a globe of the earth, and placed my finger on Cairo, Egypt, then figured out exactly where the exact other side would be, and amazingly, it was Tahiti. Of course the Sphinx sits in front of the Pyramid, which is a Lion with the head of a man, and there are some people who believe that the Pyramid may have some connection to the constellation Leo. As I had been shown that "lions" are generally seen at the entrance to sacred temples, it confirmed my thoughts, that perhaps the Pyramid was also a sacred place, or temple.

Years later, I came across some information in a book written by Drunvalo Melchizadek. In it, he states that he believes the Great Pyramid to be a major energy point on the earth, and a "male" aspect. The other side, or female side, is located somewhere in the South Pacific, on the Tahitian Island of Moorea. Once again, I was excited with the idea that I had been shown this "truth" in a vision, although I still wasn't sure why. I also came across a web article that referred to the Great Pyramid as the "Temple of the Winged Lion". Hmm!

I discovered that there are some interesting facts pertaining to the Great Pyramid, which is sometimes referred to as "Giza" or "Cheops". Interestingly, it once did have a covering on it that gave the appearance of it being made of gold, which is exactly how I saw it in my vision. The word "Py-Ra-Mid" means "fire in the middle" but the word "Ra" is also the ancient Egyptian word for "God" and some people believe that the pyramid was actually created to remind us of our connection with God. G-d in our midst?

I learned that the ancient Egyptians knew how to build monuments that were geometrically precise. If you were to measure the base of the pyramid, you would find that its overall length is twice its' height, just as the circumference of a circle. Interestingly, the Pyramid is an example of something called the "Golden Section" – a geometrical equation that is found in all forms of nature, sometimes called Phi or the Fibonacci Spiral. It contains the numbers 1.6180339887. The length of each side at the base of the pyramid is 365.2422 cubits, the exact same amount of days in the solar calendar, including the extra day that appears every 4 years.

When I woke up from another dream, a conversation was still fresh in my mind. I had been speaking to a woman, who was showing me two very large scarabs, one in each of the palms of her hands. As she turned them over, I could see their undersides, and I was asked to choose one. The underside of the one I chose was pure white, and reminded me of silk. The top of the scarab was green.

The Egyptian scarab gets its name from a beetle called "scarabeous" which has a strange habit of rolling its' dung into spherical shaped balls. The beatle was considered to be "sacred" to the ancient Egyptians, because of its ability to self-create. Just as the Egyptian Sun G-d would appear each morning, the Scarabaeus beetle would somehow seem non-existent, but would suddenly materialize out of nowhere. It was because of this, that the symbol was used to depict creation, regeneration, transformation, and resurrection. When seen in Egyptian writings, its translation is "to come into being" "to become" or "to transform".

It's common knowledge that funeral rites were a very important ceremony to the Ancient Egyptians, and scarabs had a very important and significant role. During the embalming process, the Egyptians removed most of the internal organs from the body, except for the heart, which was always left inside the body. The Ancient Egyptians believed that the heart held the mind and soul of the individual. The scarab would then be placed over the heart of the departed, to protect them and ensure that their heart would not testify against the "deceased" in the Hall of Two Truths. This was where their actions of their mortal lives would be examined before being allowed to enter the afterlife. They were usually cut from a green coloured stone, and they came to be known as "heart scarabs" which were larger in size than other scarabs, about 7.5 cm. There was also a specific prayer carved into their under side, which was "Spell 30" from the Egyptian "Book of the Dead".

"O my heart which I had from my mother, O my heart which I had upon earth, do not rise up against me as a witness in the presence of the Lord of Things; do not speak against me concerning what I have done, do not bring up anything against me in the presence of the Great God, Lord of the West".

They believed that the heart would be weighed against the "feather of truth" in the hall of Ma'at (truth) and if the heart was pure, the deceased would then be permitted into the Duat (heaven). The scarab therefore became the Egyptian symbol for rebirth. It's possible that the scarab I had been shown was one of these "heart scarabs" as it was very large and green in colour. In the dream, I had wanted this particular scarab, but I have no idea why.

I was brought back to the desert sands once again, and it seemed that I was either in some type of aircraft – or I myself was flying. Apparently I was becoming pretty good at this, as I appeared to be traveling all over the world! I could see the Golden Pyramid once again, but this time there was a building in front of it and off to the right. All of a sudden, a boat emerged, as if it had burst through the wall of the building – and it was most impressive. It too, appeared to be made of a shimmering gold, and had the most ornately designed "bow". In the middle were Golden Archways that faced several directions, engraved in Egyptian Hieroglyphics. When the boat first appeared, in the vision, an amazing feeling came over me, it was as if my heart had burst open. It was quite overwhelming.

After telling my friend, who had just returned from Egypt, about the experience, she informed me that Egyptian archeologists had actually discovered some giant boats beneath the ground in the approximate place where I had seen them in my vision. She said that according to the Egyptian philosophy, the boats were supposed to carry you across the "duat" or heavenly sky.

You can imagine how surprised I was to discover that these boats really existed. They are "Egyptian Solar Boats", as seen in the photo above. She told me that they even have a special museum built right beside the pyramids to house them. According to Egyptian beliefs, the soul of the dead accompanied the sun on its eternal journey in the Upper Waters (the heavens) around the world. A boat or at least a model of a boat was therefore included in every tomb. The above photo is from the museum. They appear very similar to reed boats, and both the stern and the bow were decorated with lotus flowers. The full sized "sacred barges" were very large, often longer than twenty metres. They were built of the best wood and decorated with precious metal. They were sometimes referred to in Egyptian literature as "August Barges" which is interesting, because it was August when I had this experience.

Another astonishing vision came in the form of a perfectly formed bird that had the most strikingly attractive head of a woman. I was completely mesmerized with her appearance and felt quite comfortable in her presence. She appeared to be very much alive, and I recall telling her how beautiful she was. Her face and hair reminded me very much of Elizabeth Taylor when she played Cleopatra. I was able to find paintings and sculptures that were made in ancient Egypt of these "part human, part bird like beings" and learned that they are known as a "Ba".

The word "Ba" actually means "soul". The Ancient Egyptians believed that a human soul was made up of five elements: The name, which they called "Ren", the personality; the "Ba", which became our identity; the life force "Ka"; the shadow, pronounced "Shwt"; as well as "Ib" known as the heart. The "Ba" is important as it is what makes an individual unique. The ancient Egyptians believed that once we had died, there was a final union between our soul and our body. The "Ba" would travel all over the earth, gathering "food" to sustain its "mummy" for the "afterlife".

At the time when I experienced it, the "Ba" appeared to me as being very real, and if I hadn't seen this impressive looking "being" I probably would have thought this only to be a myth, but now believe that it is part of some inter-dimensional truth. You can sometimes see this figure with the wings open, and it can symbolize the soul's ascension after death. I was deeply moved by all of these experiences.

Chapter 6

"Alignments"

I was overwhelmed by what was happening to me, and I suddenly felt inspired to create a painting of the "Being of Light and the Orange". I especially wanted to express the feeling that came from the Orange when it turned into the Lotus Blossom. I hadn't picked up a brush for quite a while, but suddenly felt the need to express myself! I decided to begin with a small watercolor painting of a woman emerging from a huge blossom, reaching towards an Angel. When I completed the painting, something quite extraordinary happened.

When you paint with watercolors, you use something called "gum Arabic" a substance that blocks out everything that you would like to remain white. You can paint your different colors, without having to worry about dripping them onto your white areas. It's sort of like a raincoat – it protects the areas you don't want to get wet, or change color. When you complete the painting you use a blade to scrape away the "gummed" parts, revealing the areas that are white.

I'm actually an oil painter, not a watercolorist, so when I tried to scrape the "gum Arabic" away some of the paper tore. When this happened, I noticed that the angel looked like he was wearing a crown made of two doves, and, although he was mostly blue & white, he appeared to me as pure energy, *blue and white light!* I kept staring at it, thinking to myself "this Angel looks familiar – yet this seemed impossible, how could an angel look familiar to me? " Yet, somehow I had the feeling that I *knew* this angel, and then the name "Archangel Michael" suddenly came to me. I don't know where the name came from, but it was clear as a bell, and I had never before had a name, or anything for that matter, just "pop" into my head!

I quickly searched for the old Bible that we had in the house, and started looking through it, but couldn't find the name mentioned anywhere. Was there an Angel with this name? If so, who was he? And did he wear a crown with two doves? How could I possibly know an angel? I have never been religious, so this seemed really farfetched! I went to Sunday School briefly, as a child, but only learned a little Hebrew and the odd story from the Old Testament. Angels were never mentioned, and to be honest, I never was really sure if such an entity truly existed, so the name Archangel Michael was completely foreign to me. In fact, I didn't even know what an Archangel was. My husband, who had been brought up Christian, had never heard the name either.

Later that day I had some banking to do, and as I entered the mall, I noticed some statues of angels displayed in the window of a small kiosk in front of the bank. There seemed to be quite a few, and it was obvious that this person had more than a mere interest in Angels. I knew that I couldn't share my experiences with just anyone, as most people might think I was a little strange (to say the least!). I cautiously approached the kiosk, noticing that he was in the business of making keys. I began by telling him about a couple of my dreams, and then asked him if he had ever heard of anyone by the name of "Archangel Michael". He told me that he had *definitely* heard of him, but didn't elaborate. He seemed to believe that I was going through a period of "enlightenment" and recommended a few books for me to read, especially one called "The Crystal Stair" by Eric Klein. He didn't have that particular book, but encouraged me to see if I could find it, and also to come back in a few days, as he had a couple of books about angels, that he agreed to loan me.

The next day, I happened to go into a pharmacy that had recently opened in the area called "Pharmavision". I was amused that the pharmacy included the word "vision" in it, since I was experiencing so many at the time, but synchronicity seemed to be happening in my life quite regularly now! The store sold a combination of homeopathic remedies as well as traditional pharmaceutical prescriptions. As I browsed around, I found a section of books on different types of natural healing. One book, in particular, caught my eye. The cover of the book was bright violet with silver lettering. It was called "Kryon Book II." I noticed that there was a small image of the earth in one corner with a pattern around it. I was drawn to run my finger over this image, and the strangest feeling came over me. I felt connected to it in some odd yet familiar way, but didn't know why.

I picked it up and opened randomly to a page that said:

"Dear one, if you think you have picked up this book by accident, then you really do not understand how things work."

Well, you can imagine the hair on my head almost stood straight on end! It went on to say that I should really read "Book 1" before reading this one. Well, as I have always been one not to follow rules, I figured since this was the book I had chosen, then *this* was the one I was supposed to read. Besides, they didn't even have the first book.

The author of this book stated that he was just an *ordinary* person and a total "skeptic" until he began receiving messages. I was beginning to wonder what "ordinary" people were like now, as no one seemed that way to me anymore. The main message was about "Love". Apparently Kryon is some sort of "being" who was channeled, and from what I have come to understand, channeling means that some type of angel or other entity was speaking through another's body. In this case, the person donating his body for this channeling was Lee Carroll, a human, and the author of the book. I have since discovered that there are many people who "channel" on a regular basis. While there would have been a time when I would have found this unbelievable, my mind was now being opened to many unusual things. It seemed that my world was changing quite rapidly!

Apparently, Kryon was sent here to adjust the Earth's grid, and because of this re-alignment, the earth would become more susceptible to a "higher consciousness" and awareness. At the time, I wasn't quite sure what that was supposed to mean. I eventually learned that he was referring to an energy "grid" that surrounds the earth. This "energy" had been known about for centuries, by some of the "ancient" religions, like the First Nations people, who used "Medicine Wheels" to balance this energy, and the Egyptians, who placed their temples in specific places. Even the early churches were built on power points, and, of course, the Chinese had their system of Feng Shui. Apparently the earth's grid was out of alignment, and Kryon was here to adjust it.

As I read those words, I was reminded of a dream that my sister had shared with me. She had dreamt that the earth was "off kilter". She kept trying to get people to pay attention, but no one seemed to care. She had the strong sense that there would be a disaster, and she woke up from the dream feeling very frustrated. It reminded me of what Kryon was talking about. My sister had never read the book!

The Kryon book gave a lot of unknown facts and knowledge to scientists and healers. It was very interesting, but there was a lot of information that I didn't understand. He also spoke about karma. Every thing that we say and do creates our future for us, whether it's good or bad. This is Karma. Well, Kryon was saying that we don't have to live out our karma, that we have a choice. This was explained in more detail in the first book, which I never did read, so I never did find out what the choice was! But I was excited to discover Archangel Michael's name mentioned, although, once again, I couldn't find any information about him.

Kryon stated that in 1987 there had been a question put forth to humanity, asking if there was a need for help from a higher consciousness. The answer was "yes". It seems that 1987 was a very interesting year for a great many people. I had my experience with the "Being of Light" and it was around the same time that the author of the "Angels and Oranges" book began receiving her messages. This was also the year of the "Harmonic Convergence". This was an event that was celebrated world-wide, on Aug. 16th, 1987. It was the beginning of what has come to be known as "the Galactic Alignment". People gathered at sacred sites all over the world to perform special ceremonies on that day. It was Dr. Jose Arguellas who had initiated the celebrations, as he had been studying the Mayan Calendar, and discovered an important alignment, which is supposed to complete on December 21st, 2012 on winter solstice. This is the day that the earth receives the least amount of daylight in the year. This particular day marks the end of the Mayan calendar, but many believe that this marks a whole new beginning. Some people believe that this may be the end of the world, but I believe it is the end of the world "as we see it".

I went to bed, after writing the last paragraph, and just before waking up, I had a dream in which someone was asking me to plant a special tree. They kept referring to it as the Mayan Sacred Tree. Then I heard someone say "Popul Vuh, this is true". My husband and I had been landscaping our place, so I thought that if I could find one of these trees, I would plant it. I had never heard of such a tree, but the term "Popul Vuh" seemed familiar to me, although I had no knowledge of what it meant. I am always in awe when I discover that the information I receive during my dream time is true, and I was excited to discover that there really is a Mayan Sacred Tree. I was even more surprised to discover that it was written about in a manuscript called the Popul Vuh - the very words I had heard. This document tells about their stories of creation, life and death, and a description of what they refer to as "the underworld". In the mythological section of the book, the focus is on a miraculous life-giving tree. The Ceiba tree has beautiful white flower blossoms, and the Mayan word that is found on ancient inscriptions, "sak nik' nal" (white flower object) suggests that the soul first enters the world as a white flower on the branches of the Sacred Tree, and is then clothed with flesh at birth. The Ceiba tree represents heaven and earth, the branches and leaves hold up heaven and the bottom of the trunk and roots are the earth. It is described as "a place where you will experience no pain, an abundance of delicious food and drink, a refreshing shady tree, beneath whose branches one might rest and be in peace forever." Sounds like Heaven to me! The message I received told me that the information in the Popol Vuh was true.

I was telling a friend of mine about the dream and he told me that he had a copy of the book, which he loaned to me. He also told me that he didn't think that the Ceiba Tree would survive in our northern climate. I realized that someone in my dream wanted me to include the information about this Sacred Tree in this story! Of course I was wondering what the connection was, but soon realized that it pertained to the Galactic Alignment.

The Popol Vuh is apparently the only known surviving Mayan text that had been transcribed into English. It was written in the early 1700's by Francisco Ximenez, a Franciscan monk, who received the information, shortly after the Spanish Conquest in the mid sixteen hundreds, from the original Mayan people who were of the lineage of the highland. The book lay hidden until the mid 1850's when it was discovered by Carl Scherzer, an Austrian traveler, who happened to find it hidden amongst the archives at the University of San Carlos, in Guatemala City. This book became the key to our understanding of the Mayan cosmology.

I wanted to find out more about this Sacred Tree and its connection with 2012. I came across the following:

At sunrise on December 21, 2012 for the first time in 26,000 years the Sun will rise to conjunct the intersection of the Milky Way and the plane of the ecliptic. (The sun will cross the equator of the Milky Way.) This will form a cosmic cross, which is considered to be an embodiment of the Sacred Tree, a tree remembered in all the world's spiritual traditions. Some observers say this alignment, with the heart of the galaxy in 2012, will open a channel for cosmic energy to flow through the earth, cleansing it and all that dwell upon it, raising all to a higher level of vibration. This is known as the Galactic Alignment. According to Mayan theology, the Sacred Tree grew at the centre of the cosmos at the time of creation, with all things flowing from it in four directions. Today, the Ceiba Tree is considered the physical representation of the Sacred Mayan Tree and can often be found planted in front yard of Mayan homes.

Eventually, I had the opportunity to meet Dr. Arguellas, when he was speaking in Vancouver, BC. As it turned out, I was seated directly in front of him. At the time, he was speaking about the Mayan Calendar, wanting everyone to stop using the Gregorian Calendar because it was not in tune with nature. He believed that a lot of the problems we were having on the planet were caused because of this. He explained that most calendars all over the world work in conjunction with the phases of the moon, and that it was a more natural way to live, pointing out that even women's menses cycles were every 30 days, as the moon.

That night, I went home and in the middle of the night, I was awakened. It felt like someone tapped me on my eyelid and then I was suddenly "downloaded" with Mayan hieroglyphics, which in turn prompted a series of dreams. In the first dream I was shown a pregnant bear that had no place to go. My husband and I seemed to be driving all over, looking for a place to take her, but there were no more trees left, and the children were playing in puddles wearing little "umbrella hats" as there was no natural shade to be found.

In the next dream children were playing on the lawn in front of one of their homes, when suddenly someone drove up in a car, and quickly ran up to where the children were playing, to deliver a suitcase to them. I watched as they all gathered around to watch as one of them opened the case. I was greatly upset when a bomb suddenly went off causing them great harm.

In the last dream, someone took me on an "out of my body" journey where we traveled very far. As we approached our destination I began to feel like I was choking and the skin on my arms felt like it was burning. I sensed that we were somewhere in Africa, and that the air was polluted. When I looked down I could see a huge beach covered in flamingos. Their pink feathers had turned brown and there were hundreds of them lying on the ground dead. Only two were left, and as they struggled to walk along the sand, they too looked like they were about to die.

When I woke up, I felt devastated. I really didn't know what to do with this information. I was angry and upset. If people did begin living their lives according to the Mayan calendar, or became more in tune with nature, would it create change? Would we start taking care of our forests, stop polluting the air, and end terrorist attacks? Someone from the other side was trying to get me to begin following the phases of the moon, which I try to do. I also began visualizing myself holding the earth in my hands, and surrounding her in healing energy. I shared my experience with as many people as possible, asking them to do the meditation.

Chapter 7

"A Wake-Up Call"

1995 - I could hardly wait to visit the "key man" again, anticipating that he had brought some "angel" books for me to read. When I got there, he presented me with two books that he believed I would find interesting, requesting that I read one of them first as he didn't like to be without this particular book. I was anxious to get home and begin searching for information about Archangel Michael.

The first book was also comprised of channeled messages, mostly from someone known as Hatonne. It had been written in 1991, and had a lot of predictions in it, mostly about volcanoes, flooding, war, new diseases, and also fighting over the seas. Hatonne stated that there was also going to be a war with the U.S involving other countries. As I edit this material, it is 2012, and I have witnessed many of the problems predicted. September 11th, 2001, brought forth the war on terrorism, when the twin towers were brought down. As well, "super bugs", "flesh-eating" diseases and the Ebola virus have become threats to human life, and we have had numerous volcanic eruptions, earthquakes, mass flooding, tsunamis, oil spills, as well as disputes over fish in the seas. People are upset and distraught over the mass killings of dolphins and whales and the mutilation of sharks for their fin

I read the book long into the evening, wondering about the predictions Hatonne was making, and had I been able to look ahead, would have discovered that most of his predictions were true. I found this book very frightening. I went to bed.

I can't remember the dream, but I do remember very clearly, the words spoken at the end of the dream. "They must be told that they have a curfew!" The voice was very deep and gravelly, and it felt as if it had come from the very depths of my soul, or was it the earth? I woke up in the middle of the night alarmed, wondering exactly what the words meant. Do we (humanity) have a time limit? Will the Earth be destroyed once again? I fell back to sleep.

I was unable to recall anymore dreams that night, but in the early hours of the morning I was suddenly awakened by the most beautiful Angel, and she was absolutely the most incredible thing I have ever seen – she was hovering above me, a shimmering mass of pure golden light! Her hair was floating around her as if she had entered some other dimension, and moved as hair does underwater. It too, was the color of gold – and her eyes were wide open and the colour of brilliant violet! As I gazed upon her, I noticed that she sparkled and glistened with every movement. Then, ever so gracefully, she came closer to me, and then suddenly, shouted into my ear *" This is your wake-up call!"* She flashed her name on a sign, which said

"Ariel" and then, as quickly as she had appeared, she suddenly vanished into thin air. I woke up instantly! It was 5:30 a.m. "Oh my God, I saw an angel!" I kept saying over and over in my mind. It was so beautiful, so astonishing, so majestic. I was ecstatic, to say the least. I could hardly believe it. I had always thought that angels would appear as humans with feathered wings, but Ariel appeared as pure golden light!

I practically flew out of bed and ran into the living room. My heart felt like it was dancing! I quickly looked through the book I had read before falling asleep, searching for an angel by that name. Not finding anything, I picked up the second book. "The Seven Beloved Archangels Speak" by Thomas Printz. I quickly leafed through it and then noticed a chart at the front of the book, showing an archangel associated with every day of the week. It was Friday morning. I looked down the chart and sure enough, there I found an archangel called Uriel – the spelling wasn't quite the same, but for me, it was close enough! (I discovered that Ariel can be spelt many different ways, Ariel, Auriel, and Uriel.) I learned that Ariel was the ancient named used for Jerusalem, and it means "Lion of God" or "Lion of Light". Ari is the Hebrew word for Lion and El means G-d or Light. I wondered if there was any connection between the drawing of the "winged lion" I had previously been shown, and Ariel.

In the section about Friday's Angel, I read that Ariel is the Spirit of Peace and Grace. The article went on to explain that the archangels work together with Lord Michael. It was here that I learned that the

"Lord Michael" they were referring to was none other than "Archangel Michael" also known as the Prince of Angels and the protector of humanity, as well as the guardian of the Elemental Kingdom and Angelic Host. He is considered to be the greatest of all of the angels, and written about in the Judaic, Islamic, and Christian teachings.

While reading about the archangels, I came across some information about an amethyst ring. I had been wearing one since December in 1994, when I had been particularly drawn to it, while vacationing in Mexico. I had been wearing it ever since then. The book said that during the times of Atlantis, only a Priest or Priestess of Zadkiel would dare to wear such a ring. The statement made me question whether Atlantis had truly existed, and I also wondered who Zadkiel was. I discovered that he was the Archangel of Mercy. I had been wearing an Amethyst ring for several months, but couldn't imagine that I could be any type of priestess, but then again, several months prior, I never would have thought any of these experiences to be possible. Everything seemed so incredible to me. I don't think I could possibly explain to anyone the amaze or awe that I felt that day. It was July 28th, 1995, that Ariel appeared to me. I remember it well, because it was the day before my birthday.

Eventually, I was recommended a book called "Mahatma I & II", by Brian Grattan, which also had a section about Archangels. It was there that I learned more about Ariel, I read that she has "directorship" over every artist that has ever lived, and that art is basically a reflection of the wonderful gifts we have been given by our creator. As well, Ariel can assist with personal relationships, helping to restore harmony between couples, which became a great help to me! I began calling for her assistance, whenever I felt the need, and amazingly, it worked. In the Mahatma book, Ariel was referred to as being male, yet her appearance to me was clearly female. I discovered that angels are basically "androgynous"- both "male and female" together in one body. Although they may appear to look masculine or feminine, they are androgynous.

In Ted Andrews "Animal-Speak" book he states that Ariel is the angel of the Earth, and the very same one that spoke to Shirley MacLean throughout her pilgrimage through Spain. A few years later I was able to find some more information about this beautiful angel through the internet, and what really amazed me, was when I learned that her "Celebration of Feast Day" is July 28th the very same day she had appeared to me!

Later that morning, after seeing Ariel, I went down to visit my sister-in-law. I loved taking walks down there, because of how quiet that area around there is. You can actually hear the sounds of birds and crickets. I dropped in to visit them, and was dying to tell them about Ariel, but I figured that they might think I was crazy, so decided not to. Just then I glanced down at the newspaper on the table, and noticed the "Vancouver Province." On the front was a large photo of the NHL player Gino Odjick. The headlines stated that he had experienced a "vision" of a Native Woman riding a horse, who had given him an important message. The article stated that he had been on a drinking binge, ending up in such a state that he was hospitalized. It was while unconscious that he had a vision. A woman appeared to him, telling him that he was supposed to stop drinking and set a good example for the Native People.

I was excited and relieved to see that I wasn't the only one who was having strange but wonderful experiences. I had been questioning my sanity, but after reading the article, I figured that if someone famous was willing to publicly announce that he had such an experience, then I could certainly talk about mine. I shared my experience with my sister-in-law about seeing Ariel. I was quite surprised that she didn't think I was crazy. She told me that she also had an unusual experience while driving home one night, from the states. Both her and my brother-in-law had actually seen a spaceship. At the time, it seemed odd that they were talking about UFO's, when I was talking about angels. I really didn't see any connection between the two, but I was glad that they felt open enough to share the experience with me.

As I walked home later, I kept thinking about Ariel. I could still hardly believe that I had such an experience, and how lucky I was to have had a visit from her. I was trying to recall if anyone else I knew had actually seen an angel. Then I remembered that my husband's father used to see angels. I had never had the opportunity to meet him, as he had passed away long before my husband and I had ever met.

On one occasion, my husband's little sister Elsie went "missing" when she was only about two years old. She had wandered away from their farm, and people from all around were searching the area for her. My brother-in-law Jim was sitting in the horse and buggy with his father as they were driving along an old dirt road through a forest looking for her, when suddenly his father pulled the reins for the horses to stop. Although Jim was unable to see anything, his father said that he had seen a boy that was blue, and called him an angel. He had darted right in front of the buggy and ran into the forest. His father immediately climbed down, running into the forest after the blue angel. Instantly the "blue boy" vanished, but amazingly he had led him right to his little girl. When I heard the story, I truly believed that it was surely a miracle!

My mind wandered back to the present, and I began to wonder what had prompted my visit from an angel, and especially about my "wake up call". I wondered if it had anything to do with my "mission" and if so, what could be important enough to warrant a visit from an angel. I certainly didn't feel all that special, and I knew that I hadn't achieved anything important in my life. After telling my husband about the visit, he said that I was either "going crazy" and would end up in a mental institution, or that I was going to die! Apparently Elsie, my husband's little sister who had been found in the forest, died only a few years later when she was only seven years old. She had told her family that she had seen angels chasing after her shortly before. Many years have gone by since Ariel's visit, and I'm still here to talk about it.

It certainly seemed odd that it would be happening to me, because I certainly was no angel. In fact, many times I considered myself to be the "black sheep" of my family. When people meet me now, they find that hard to believe. But during my teenage years, I gave everyone the impression that I was "wild and crazy" and because of that, my teachers gave me a hard time. Although I didn't think I was all that bad, I was a bit of a "rebel" and caused "many a heartache" for my parents while I was growing up. When people would comment about how quiet I was, my mother would often say "still waters run deep". I was married in my early twenties, got divorced, and then remarried. I smoked a lot of hash and grass in my early twenties, and was even arrested for verbally assaulting a police officer while in Israel. (I spent three days in prison for that, but luckily for me, the charges were eventually dropped.) I never did well scholastically either, as I seemed to "day-dream" constantly, and when I consciously returned to class, I had no idea as to what was going on. I eventually did graduate, but it was by the skin of my teeth. I find it ironic that people who meditate, try to clear their mind. I seemed to be able to do this quite naturally, but unfortunately, I did it all the way through school!

But, my life had changed. As a mother of three, I loved my kids like crazy, and while I can't say that I was the best mother, I certainly wasn't the worst. My life was really quite tame, and other than the occasional glass of wine, my behavior was pretty good, compared to years before! I couldn't for the life of me figure out what I had a done to deserve a visit from this beautiful angel? But, it was exciting, and I wondered what it was that I was supposed to do. What was it that I was "awakened" for?

Chapter 8

"Angels & UFO's?"

I developed an incredible thirst for knowledge, so I returned to the bookstore once again, and this time I was able to find "The Crystal Stair", the book which had been recommended by the man at the kiosk. Even though I never really got to know him very well, this gentleman that I began referring to as the "key man" played a key role in my "awakening" experience. By lending to me his books on angels, and recommending several other books to read, he had unlocked a door for me, which allowed me to step into a new and very unique journey. When I began to read "The Crystal Stair" I discovered some messages that had supposedly been channeled from Archangel Michael. If I hadn't experienced the "angelic visits" myself, I probably wouldn't have believed a lot of what I was reading. But I have to say, I was actually relieved to know that there were others that appeared to be in contact with the angelic realm, and that, in fact, I hadn't lost my mind.

There were several "channeled" messages from several beings, one was someone by the name of Sananda. I was surprised to learn that this was actually another name used by Jesus. As well, there were messages from a being known as Ashtar, who was in charge of a group of beings known as the "Ashtar Command". From what I understood, they were on a spaceship. I began to feel as if I was taking part in a "Starwars" episode! I recalled that this group had also been mentioned in the Kryon book. I soon learned that the "Command" consisted of a group of beings that visit the earth quite often and are here to help us. This really started the wheels rolling in my head. From all the books I had been reading, it appeared to me that this world was a part of a very complex universe, and that we are one small part of it.

The "Crystal Stair" was written by Erik Klein, and the main subject appeared to be "ascension". From what I understood, these "beings" were encouraging its' readers to "ascend" and then return to become teachers. On looking up the word "ascension" I could only find reference to Christ's body ascending into heaven for forty days, after his resurrection.

I recalled that when my sister-in-law had mentioned seeing a UFO, I hadn't felt that there was any sort of connection between UFO's and angels. But after reading "The Crystal Stair" it seemed that there was, and that they worked together. I was reminded about another book I had read about a year prior, which was written by an acquaintance. She was a UFO artist and writer by the name of Shirle (pronounced Shir-lay) Kline-Carsh. The book she wrote was called "Permutation, A True UFO story". Her story was quite unusual, but she claimed that it was true.

Highly respected in the UFO community, Shirle has been invited to speak all over the world. She explained in her book that she met a man over twenty years ago, who appeared to her as being human, but told her that he was really not from this planet. He gave her some plates to keep that have foreign writing inscribed on them. The writing has never been deciphered, but some people believe that it might be similar to the writing of Atlantis. Shirle keeps the plates in a safety deposit box, because after having them analyzed, she learned that they are made of 24 carat gold. She was told that there are eight other people around the world who also have sets of these plates, and that eventually they will all meet. (It will be interesting to see what happens when all the plates come together.) She also claims that this "being" told her that she is the captain of a spaceship. Shirle is always telling me that everyone thinks she's crazy, but she doesn't care. I decided to look through her book again to see if there was anything mentioned about the Ashtar Command. As I skimmed through the book, I noticed that they had been briefly acknowledged, but something else caught my attention. I didn't recall reading this part before, but there it was:

When Shirle's mother was giving birth to her, she was having a hard time during delivery. Suddenly a "Being of Light" appeared next to her mother, offering her a glass of "orange" juice. Ah ha! Another "angel and orange" experience. Just as I had been visited by a "being of light" and was given an orange, Shirle's mother also had a "visitor" who had given her *Orange* juice. Both angelic beings had appeared at "trying" moments in our lives. I had been feeling disillusioned with my life, and Shirle's mom was having difficulty giving birth. The Being of Light told her that her baby would be an artist, so Shirle's mom had her taking piano lessons for many years, thinking she would grow up to be a great musician. Well Shirle is an artist, but a painter not a musician! I found it interesting that her name was similar to the author of the Crystal Stair in that they both share the same family name "Klein". I decided to call Shirle, and tell her about all the visions I was having. "Oh, you woke up!" she said, and invited me to meet her for lunch.

The Crystal Stair had some beautiful meditations given by Archangel Michael and Sananda. I began practicing one of the meditations in the book. It had been "channeled" by Archangel Michael, and in it, you would enter a "pyramid" asking for protection from your guides and angels, and then call for your "light body". Then you would travel inside this "pyramid of light" to a beautiful island made of crystal beaches. Each of the beaches were made of different colours, which corresponded to the chakras of the body. (At the time, I had no knowledge of chakras, but later learned that we have seven of these "energy gates" or "wheels" within our body.)

Shirle mentioned that I should take a second look at some of my artwork, to see what I had been creating. About a year prior, I had painted a series of large, mixed media, paintings. The series sold extremely well, but I still had a few that I had kept for myself. After taking another look at them, I couldn't help but notice that they looked exactly like the crystal beaches I had "seen" during my meditation. I began to think about whether such places truly existed, and if somehow I had visited these other dimensions. Is it possible that somewhere deep inside my mind, their memory left such an impression, that I was able to recreate them on canvas? Hmm!

Chapter 9

"Ashtar & Noah"

After searching through Shirle's book, I wasn't able to find anything more about Ashtar. I decided to ask when I went to sleep, who Ashtar was and if he was perhaps one of God's messengers. That night, I was shown what looked like Noah's Ark, and then I was shown a spaceship. Below and to the left I noticed the name "Noah" with a number next to it, and then Ashtar's name directly below Noah's with a number next to his. (Apparently, everything in the cosmos is based on mathematics and we all have numbers.) I couldn't recall if the numbers were the same, but nevertheless, I was shown they had a comparable mission. Although Noah's Ark and the spaceship I was shown, didn't look anything alike, I sensed that they served a similar purpose. In the next scene, I discovered myself *inside the space ship heading towards the light.* I seemed to be alone.

The experience reminded me of a mysterious event that had happened several years prior. Not a dream or vision, but something that happened during my waking hours. I remember being in my home, when I suddenly heard a large thud. I thought someone had come into the house, but didn't hear anything more, so I didn't pay too much attention to it. A little while later I went into the living room and discovered three books lying on the floor next to a large wooden carving of a fish. The bookshelf held at least a hundred or more books, consisting of many different subjects, so it was strange that those particular books along with the fish, had fallen onto the floor. It was almost as if someone had pulled them off of the bookshelf and thrown them there, to get my attention. The first book was called "Listen to the Master" and I can't remember what the name of the second book was, except that it was more like a pamphlet. They had been sitting on the shelf for years. I glanced through the books to see what they were about, and found it curious that the second one seemed to refer to the Earth as a "Spaceship". The third book was an antique Bible that I had. My husband had salvaged it from several other books that had been thrown out by a friend of his. But here it was lying on the floor with the other books. The whole episode seemed very strange, especially since they were lying right beside the fish, a symbol that used to represent spirituality, and more commonly Christianity. At the time, I found it unusual that a "spaceship" appeared to be mentioned in the booklet, which had originally been left at my door by Jehovah Witnesses, several years before. This was the only time I had ever come across any reference to a spaceship in a religious text. The vision of Noah's Ark and Ashtar's spaceship, reminded me of the experience.

The Bible had an inscription on the inside cover describing that it had been given as a gift to the owner from his mother in 1882. It was lying face down with the back cover opened, and on the inside was a handwritten message in the most beautiful script, "And as it w as in the days of Noe, so shall it be also in the days of the son of Mary." I remember at the time, wondering what the message meant. Had she been referring to the time of Noah? When would the "days of the Son of Mary" be? Would that be now? Were they referring to a time when Christianity would be strong? In the story of Noah, G-d had been unhappy because there was too much evil on the earth, and informed Noah to build a huge Ark to bring aboard all the animals and plants, as there was going to be a huge flood. The Ark had to be built to God's exact specifications, and each of the animals had to be in pairs, male and female. Were we going to go through a similar experience? After the flood, Noah had been shown a Rainbow, representing God's promise to never again destroy the earth by water. There are several Christian faiths that consider this flood was the earth's baptism; and that 'baptism by fire' is to be the next event in the earth's evolution. Even though we seemed to be experiencing a lot of "evil" on the earth, I still have to say that I hope this latter part will not turn out to be true, if it is to destroy the earth!

I have since seen several documentaries on TV about Noah's Ark, and it is believed by some, that it is embedded in the glacial ice of Mount Ararat, Turkey. I also came to believe that possibility many years ago, while traveling through Greece in 1973. I was in a small village called Meteora, which had several minute monasteries that had been built, and sat perched, on the very tops of "dome shaped" mountains. They had been built in the fourteenth century, and the priests lived inside these monasteries their whole lives completely in solitary. Their food was sent up to them in baskets, which they lowered every day. As we approached this tiny village the highway twisted and turned, and as you gazed upon this cluster of strange shaped mountains, set amongst the Greek countryside, it gave the illusion of a Disneyland castle. I later learned that during the Dark Ages, it was due to places like Meteora, and other isolated monasteries located in other parts of the earth, that sacred art and knowledge were preserved.

It was fortunate for me, that just when I arrived at Meteora, they were in the process of building a roadway to reach these little churches, and I was one of the first foreigners to ever step inside one of them. I recall a priest showing me a cross, made of wood with a figure of Jesus carved on it. The priest told me that the wood had actually been made from a piece of Noah's Ark. As we walked down the mountain, I also noticed that there were little shells and fossils embedded throughout the mountain. I had truly been given the impression that the story of Noah's Ark could possibly be true. I have since learned that many "philosophies" throughout the world speak of the Great Flood. My mind, once again recalled the dream I had about the curfew. As I lay in bed that night I wondered what all the messages were about. Was Ashtar's spaceship going to pick up different species of Earth to save us from a disaster, like Noah's Ark had supposedly done before?

When I finally fell asleep I could see a lot of angels, and a winged white horse flying towards me. After sharing the experience with a friend, she said that Pegasus guards our spirit through its journeys on the astral plane, and points us in the right direction." After what I was experiencing, I hoped she was right!

The next morning, was my birthday, July 29th, I drove into Vancouver to have lunch with my mother. Although it felt odd sharing these experiences with my mother, I told her about the "Wake up call" from Ariel and the visions of Egypt. My mother has always had a strong belief in God, and she also believed in astrology, as well as ESP, but I wondered if she would think that her daughter had "gone of the deep end". She seemed to accept it fairly well, and was smiling when she handed me a birthday card. Inside there was a little angel pin!

Chapter 10

"Champagne and Roses"

I was working as a realtor, and it was the summer of 1995. The real estate market was really soft, and I hadn't had a sale for quite a while. One of the books I had been reading had said that if you were in need of financial assistance, you could ask for a "direct source of income" before going to sleep at night, which I did. Never in a million years, would I have believed what happened next!

The following morning, my husband Phil got up and went out to his shop at the back of our property. I had my 2 year old niece in the bathtub, when suddenly Phil came running back into the house very excited. He kept saying "Hurry up, come on out, or you'll miss it! A hot air balloon is landing right on our property!" I quickly wrapped my niece in a towel, and carrying her in my arms, ran out to watch. This beautiful brightly colored yellow and red striped balloon gently floated across the sky, and landed ever so gently in our yard. At the same time, a man in a SUV drove into our driveway, rolling down his window and apologizing, to us, while telling us that he was the owner of the balloon. He explained that there didn't seem to be anywhere else to land, as we were the only "small acreage" in the area. Of course, we didn't mind, in fact we were really excited and thrilled about it.

I wasn't aware that when balloons land, it's customary to have a special ceremony, so I was quite surprised to see a small table suddenly appear, along with some glasses and a bottle of Champagne. They invited us to celebrate along with them, and here I was drinking champagne first thing in the morning. What a surprise! – It felt like the angels had sent me a giant balloon and champagne for my birthday. How incredible was this? It was a day late, but better late than never!

We stood around drinking and talking to the balloon people. There were two riders, the balloonist, and the owner who had was in the truck. I'm not sure what I was thinking (maybe the champagne had something to do with it) but I kept associating the owner with Ashtar, and even called him that by mistake! Of course, I quickly apologized saying that he reminded me of someone by that name. It turned out that when I told them I was a realtor, the owner said he was interested in purchasing a home, and understood that he needed a realtor. He even knew which home he wanted to buy (he had previously landed on that particular property too!) Well who would have believed it? Here I had asked for a direct source of income, and a hot air balloon dropped right out of the sky into my yard, with the owner needing a realtor!

Over the next few weeks, I got to know the "balloon people" quite well, and sensed that they were very caring people. They even invited me for dinner one night. I don't know why, but I decided to tell them about my beautiful Angel Ariel. They were so interested and thankful that I had shared my story with them. Then the owner told me about his own extraordinary experience. He explained that a woman had been visiting him fairly often. I sensed he was talking about an apparition, and he said that he looked forward to her visits, which lasted over a year. During that time she had only spoken to him, except for her very last visit, when she revealed herself to him, and she was dressed in blue. Amazingly, she had been telling him about a new way to eliminate toxic waste, which was natural and environmentally safe. "Kryon" had mentioned in the book that many people would be receiving messages about healing and information would be given to scientists that would prove to be beneficial to the earth and humanity. It was as if I was being shown that this information was truly happening. I was so mesmerized by his story that I forgot to ask who she was or what she looked like. Even though I come from a Jewish background, and not Catholic, I somehow had a strong sense that the woman who had visited him, was "Mother Mary" – although I can't be sure. I am uncertain as to why I would think that, but I just had this "knowingness" which seemed to becoming a part of my life. Unfortunately I never did find out who this woman actually was. I had sensed that if he had wanted to share that information, he would have done so, and I didn't want to intrude on his privacy.

So much was happening in such a very short amount of time that I was overwhelmed. I seemed to crave the feeling of being close to nature. I would often walk down to the area where my sister-in-law lived. On one of my walks I met a woman who lived in the vicinity. We stopped and chatted for a while, but I really didn't want to talk to anyone. I just wanted to be alone and experience total peace and quiet in a natural surrounding, so I went home. Ironically, the very next day, after walking down to the same spot, as I stood there gazing at some of the horses, the same woman appeared out of nowhere. She had a five-dollar bill in her hand and asked if it belonged to me. She said that she had found it on the ground and wondered if I had lost it. I assured her that it wasn't mine, as I didn't bring a purse or any money with me.

The following day I returned and once again was approached by this woman. This time she told me that a cougar had been spotted in the area about an hour before. She had called the SPCA to see if they could catch the animal and move it to an area where it wouldn't be so close to the public. She was wondering if I had seen them arrive yet.

In her next breath, she asked if I wanted to walk down the path where she had seen the cougar. I said, "sure" - and we walked all the way down the road and back. I didn't have any fear at all about running into the cougar, as by this time I truly believed that I was being watched over and protected by God's Angels. As I walked home, I couldn't help thinking that as much as I tried to experience some peace and quiet, the same woman kept interrupting me. That night I decided to ask why this woman kept "appearing" when all I wanted was to be alone with nature.

I had a dream: My mother was visiting me when there was a knock on my front door (which is unusual, because everyone usually enters my home from the kitchen entrance). I answered the door to discover someone delivering a huge bouquet of roses to me. I mean it was absolutely massive. I had never seen such a large bouquet, the roses must have spread out to about three feet in width! Directly behind this bouquet was a significant sized glass container. It was about rectangular in shape, which was divided into smaller cubed boxes. Inside each box there was a bouquet of roses.

In the dream, my mother said "Oh your Uncle must have sent you some flowers for your birthday." I said "No Mom, there is only one person that would send me roses like that." She asked "Who would that be?" I said "That would be God!!" I heard a voice say "You passed your tests!"

I woke up with those words on my mind. I wondered what "tests" they were referring to, and remembered my question before falling asleep. I then realized that the woman that kept intruding on my "sacred space" had been sent to test me. First for my honesty, and then my belief in God. I had told her that the five dollar bill didn't belong to me, when I could have easily claimed it to be mine, and my belief in G-d was strong enough not to fear the wild cougar. I guess we're being tested all the time. Perhaps life is one big test. If so, there are many tests I have failed, but perhaps I was being given a second chance.

Chapter 11

"A Sacred Place"

It was late August in 1995.   I was still practicing the pyramid meditation given by Archangel Michael. I would do this while I lay in bed at night and would fall asleep, but in the morning, I seemed to remember everything that happened. This time, as I had entered the meditation, I heard a voice telling me that Sananda (Jesus) was going to be on my island. I walked around the island visiting each of the different coloured beaches, and eventually saw a man walking towards me with his hands stretched out, just like Jesus on the cross. As I got closer, I was surprised to see that it wasn't Sananda but my neighbour Don. I thought to myself "This is really weird, surely Don couldn't be Sananda."

I was living on a small piece of acreage, and Don parked his camper at the back of our property. He also restores cars, and was doing some restoration work on old Mustang that belonged to my brother-in-law, Jim. So I would see Don almost everyday, as he would come in for coffee and sit and gab with my husband and Jim all the time, mostly about hunting and other subjects that I had no interest it. Don was living (on and off) with a woman named Cindy that lived in the townhouse development next to our property. Cindy kept breaking up with him but he kept "hanging in there". I often thought that he would be better off just forgetting about her, but he kept going back into the relationship. I wondered why I was shown Don as Sananda, was there a lesson to be learned? The only thing that I could figure out was that Don was showing Cindy unconditional love, as Jesus does (or Sananda). The vision made me look at Don in a different light, and I tried to make more of an effort to listen to what he had to say. I guess I was also being shown that we must treat everyone as if they are someone special, since we don't know who they really are.

The dreams and visions continued and the following night I dreamt that I was inside a small room. There was a very large book on the table and it seemed very old, as the pages were yellowed and some of them were falling out. I don't know what the book was about, but I had the impression that it was very important. It appeared to be records of some type. Then I was shown a huge map. Strangely, I don't remember who it was that was showing me these things. They unrolled the map and told me that this was a map of the New World. It was very large and took up the entire size of the table. I remember it seemed quite plain at first, and I can't remember what else I was shown. Then I seemed to be sitting on a bench and a bottle of perfume was beside me, tipped over with the perfume pouring out. I was holding my eyes, saying "you have spilt too much perfume and my eyes are burning". The next thing I knew I was dropped off in the middle of a road somewhere in the country. When I told a friend about the dream, she said that I was talking in "parables". She said that Jesus used to talk in parables, and she thought that perhaps "the map of the New World was too beautiful for my mortal eyes".

That morning Don came over quite early, about eight o'clock in the morning. As I walked into the kitchen, he said "Come on, I want to show you something." I followed him out the door and around towards the back of the house. He was about six feet in front of me, and as I followed him, my eyes started burning because the light around him was so bright. I actually had to cover my eyes from the brightness. Were my eyes burning because they were sensitive from what I had seen in my dream, or was it from the light around Don? I didn't know, and couldn't tell. I watched as he went over to a tree and took three little baby birds out of their nest and placed them at his feet. He took the fourth bird and placed it in his hand. He carefully spread the baby bird's wings out, showing me how delicately they were developing. I said "Don, what are you doing? The mother won't fed them if you touch them." He assured me that they were fine and informed me that he had been touching them ever since they were born, and that the mother bird was still feeding them. I could see that Don had a lot of love for these little birds, and he had wanted to share this experience with me. I looked at the tiny little bird with only half of its' feathers on, and with all that was happening to me, I couldn't help but feel like I to, was one of God's little birds or perhaps "angel" with only half of my feathers on! I guess to that little winged creature, Don was like Sananda. I had definitely seen Don in another light, and it was very bright! He gently placed each of the birds back in their nest.

That evening, during my meditation, when I visited my "beach" I was surprised to be greeted by Elvis Presley! Although I have always thought he was a great singer, I would never really call myself an Elvis fan, so I was really surprised when he appeared to me. He told me that part of his work was to "guide and help people get to their sacred place".

After being greeted by Elvis, I continued on my path and could see Sananda in the distance, and this time it was really him. He was walking towards me, with his arms stretched out, and he looked so handsome. He was dressed in a gown made of hundreds of pure white feathers, and his hair was shoulder length and golden. He appeared to be very gracious, gentle and loving. Strangely, as he approached me, he seemed to step inside my body, and I had the sense that our bodies merged together.

Being Jewish, it seemed odd to me that I was having visions of Jesus/Sananda. While I had never really thought too much about it, I believed that Jesus did exist and that he was a very special being, but knew that the Jewish people had never really accepted him as the Messiah. While growing up, I lived in a predominantly Christian area, and was one of the very few Jewish children in my school. I found it difficult to understand why almost everyone else used to celebrate Christmas except for us. It was bewildering to me that all of the schools would put on Christmas plays, and the stores were all decorated for Christmas, but they didn't do anything for Chanukah, or celebrations of any other religions, for that matter. I remember asking my mother when I was a child why we didn't celebrate Christmas. She told me that Christianity was actually based on the Jewish religion, and I was really surprised when she told me that Jesus was Jewish. She explained that the Jews had been waiting for the Messiah to arrive for thousands of years. I asked her if she thought that Jesus really had been the Messiah. I remember my mother saying that with so many people believing in him, and all the miracles he had performed, that it was quite possible.

Of course, I wondered why the Jewish people didn't accept Jesus as the Messiah. My mother explained that during those times, there had been many people that had proclaimed to be the Messiah, but they turned out not to be true. She went on to say "If the Messiah appeared on earth today and people started introducing him as the Christ, how many people do you think would actually believe it? The majority of people in all probability would not accept him. They would have to personally experience his presence, or know someone they trusted that had actually seen or felt his presence and witnessed some miracles. They would probably say that he was an imposter. The people that really accepted Jesus were probably those that actually saw him perform miracles, or had been healed by him. Most of those people, and many of the Apostles, were as a matter of fact, Jewish. The majority of the people probably didn't get to see those miracles, and so they didn't believe that he truly was the long awaited Messiah.

As I was thinking about my mother's words, the phone rang. She called to tell me that there was an interesting show on T.V. about angels. I turned on the T.V. and began watching. I was excited to see that the show was about Archangel Michael and I was able to learn more about Him. A famous healer on that show said that he always called Michael to help him while performing healings on people. Others mentioned that if you were ever in trouble that all you had to do was call for him and you would be protected. Later, I was told that the Jehovah Witnesses actually believe that Jesus was Michael. Of course, I don't know if that is true!

I was surprised to learn that there are Jewish prayers invoking Michael for protection, along with Gabriel, Raphael, and Ariel. The name Michael in Hebrew means "Who is as G-d" and he carries a "Sword of Light" that has Hebrew letters on it. Michael is an Angel known not only to Christians and Jews, but to the Muslim people, as well.

In another dream I was shown a roll of white tape. Then the top layer was peeled back and the tape inside was all black. I felt that this was a warning of sorts. I believe that they were showing me never to judge a book by its cover, or that all is not what it may appear to be.

The next thing I knew, I found myself inside a beautiful white house. I was climbing up a circular stairway, when a very handsome man came partway up and invited me to dance. I went down the stairs and joined him. The room was quite beautiful, everything was white, including the fireplace, the walls, and the carpet. Even this handsome man was dressed totally in white wearing a tuxedo. As we danced together, he suddenly began groping and touching me in such a way that felt very uncomfortable, and as I tried to push him away, I became aware that his appearance was changing and he was beginning to look more and more unattractive. I suddenly felt like I was dancing with the "Devil" himself. I called for Michael and instantly found myself floating with Michael on my left and some "cherubs" on my right. They were forming a spiral leading up towards the light. The roll of tape was obviously a warning. It seemed that looks can be deceiving, and that I shouldn't trust everyone.

Then I was taken through a series of the most amazing beautiful places. They looked like huge temples or churches, each was more beautiful than the next. At the beginning of this "tour" I found myself inside a beautiful blue and white dome. It was very peaceful there, and I felt that this was my particular "place of peace". Upon returning to the blue dome, there were black swastikas floating around inside my temple. In the dream, I said "All that are not of

God's highest will, must leave!" They vanished instantly. Shortly after I was shown a drawing of three circles, the smallest in the centre and each one larger on the outside, and it appeared as the drawing of the inside of a dome. Beneath the dome was a drawing of an Angel with a sword fighting a Dragon.

The next morning I discussed the dream with my husband. He said that the reason that I dreamt that was because the night before I had seen on the news that someone had put swastikas on a sign that the Jewish community had displayed. The sign was showing that they were building a Community Centre, which was going to be open to everyone. My husband said that the news broadcast probably triggered off the dream. I accepted this reasoning.

About a week later, it mentioned on the news that a member of the KKK who was quite high up in the organization was missing. I said to my husband "Don't they call the high priest of the KKK, the Grand Dragon?" He said "You're right, they do." I looked at my husband and said "Maybe my angel got him!" I later came across an illustration of Archangel Michael fighting a Dragon with his sword. I was quite amazed that I had been shown all this in a dream, and it seemed so extraordinarily coincidental.

Chapter 12

"Angels, Eagles & Ascension"

When I first became a realtor in 1993, I started working with a real estate company that offered on-going classes, and I really liked the teacher. The whole time I was there, all of the classes were about selling real estate. But in 1995, the instructor suddenly offered a very different class called "The Master Key". I signed up for it, not realizing that it was metaphysical. I know it seems strange that this would be offered in a real estate office, but it was. There were about six people in the class, and I joined after it had already started, and never did finish the course, so I wasn't able to find out what "The Master Key" actually was.

It was while taking this class that I first heard about many different spiritual ideas, and where I first heard about "Reiki", the Japanese "hands on" healing technique. I guess the old saying "when the student is ready, the teacher appears" is true. Whoever would believe that a real estate office would be offering metaphysical classes! I had joined the class about a month before I began having the visions.

Almost two months went by and for personal reasons I hadn't been in the office. It was during this time that Ariel, my beautiful Angel, brought me my "Wake up Call". About a week after that experience, I called Dianna, the woman who was facilitating "The Master Key" classes and asked her if we could meet for lunch. She asked me what I wanted to talk about. I told her "I had a visit from an Angel." She seemed quite surprised, and said "That's really incredible, because we have been taking a rest from "The Master Key" sessions and our meeting today was to be all about angels." She asked me to come and share my experience, which I did! It felt odd telling people about what was happening to me, because I worried that they might think I had "lost it". Of course, all the people attending these classes are interested in spirituality, and they were all very fascinated with my story. I even told Mike, the owner of the Real Estate company, about my experiences and he was quite comfortable with it. I wasn't sure if he believed me, because he didn't look like I had told him anything "out of the ordinary", but then he told me that his wife, Linda, also saw angels, and that it had been his idea to bring "The Master Key" class into the office.

After the meeting, I went for lunch with one of the other realtors. I was feeling really "light-headed" after talking about my experiences. I didn't realize it at the time, but just talking about these experiences was putting me into an altered state. I went into the washroom to splash some cold water on my face, and when I looked in the mirror, I could only see part of my face.   I remember reading in James Redfield's "Celestine Prophecy" how people could disappear and reappear. I laughed, and thought to myself "Holy smokes, I'm going to disappear in the washroom, and all they will find is my messy purse! I quickly went back and sat down with my friend Sara. I looked over at her and noticed that I could only see half of her face too, the other half appeared as millions of miniscule stars, and this was happening all the way down her arm. I put on my sunglasses to cut out the brightness. I looked around the room to see if anyone else seemed to be experiencing any of this, but I didn't notice anything unusual. Sara looked at me and burst out laughing "Why are you wearing your glasses when it is so dark in here!" she said. "Oh, my eyes are bothering me" I said.   I was at a loss for words. How could I tell her that half of her body was disappearing right in front of me?

That night I had another vision It looked like a huge grassy area, like a valley – all around the valley were bushes. In the middle of the sky, facing me, was a large face. He looked to be around 50 years old, and was quite handsome with grey hair, a small "goatee" beard and a moustache. All around the face, were spaceships, hovering. In the dream, I also felt that I knew where the area was that this was taking place. It was close to the border between Canada and the US, outside of Vancouver, British Columbia, in a valley called Semiahmoo, about a fifteen minute drive from where I lived, but probably seconds in a spaceship! I woke up wondering what this dream was about. Were they showing me that they were close by?

About a year later I was given a book called "The Lords of the Seven Rays: Mirror of Consciousness" by Mark L. Prophet and Elizabeth Clare Prophet. It was in this book that I came across a photograph of the man I had seen in the vision. It was the face of Saint Germaine, who is known as "The Keeper of the Violet Flame" and an Ascended Master. I have also seen paintings of the same face in which it is shown in the sky, which tells me that others have had a similar vision to mine.

I still wasn't sure what an Ascended Master was, but knew that Jesus had ascended, so I assumed that he was part of this group, and I was correct. Each of these masters was born in exactly the same way as you and I were, and each of them also lived many lives. They became Ascended Masters because they were able to learn how to master their lives. In each incarnation, they were able to fulfill their mission on earth, while fully becoming an expression of the purest form of love. Once they completed their mission, they were rewarded the highest victory, which is Ascension. I was happy to learn exactly what ascension was, and apparently it is the integration and full embodiment of our "beings" into the Light of our Higher Selves, although I wasn't sure what the term "Higher Selves" meant. I later learned that it is "that part of ourselves that is connected to God" our cosmic consciousness, our "Godselves". I also learned that these Masters will assist those of us on earth that are ready to accomplish this same goal, and will continue to do so until "all" are received into the light. This seemed like quite an achievement, and of course, I wondered if this had anything to do with my "mission". I found it difficult to comprehend that I, or anyone I know for that matter, would be able to accomplish such a feat.

I discovered that there are many Ascended Masters, and Mother Mary and Buddha are also part of this group. These "Rays of Light" or Higher Conscousness" come in every colour of the rainbow, and each have specific meanings. There are Seven Lords of the Rays, with Saint Germaine being Lord of the Seventh Ray, and the Keeper of the Violet Flame. He had many lifetimes, but some of his more famous ones were Christopher Columbus and Merlin "the magician".

At a certain point in our life, we may be invited to visit these Lords' etheric retreats, in order to review our past lives, and to learn what could be causing certain experiences in our present. At this time, our Divine Blueprint would be revealed to us by Saint Germaine, showing us what is still to be completed. It is through the Violet Flame that we are able to transmute any negative karma that we may have created within this lifetime, and past lives, in hopes that we choose to complete our mission.

A few days later after seeing the face in the sky, I had another vision. I was shown a light grey eagle, and a few minutes later it looked more like a spaceship. Below was a huge light-blue angel, which was much larger than the craft. This angel was so magnificently large that it totally filled the sky. I had the distinct feeling that this was Archangel Michael. The clouds seemed to clear instantly to reveal the whole sky filled with tiny white Eagles on each side of the Blue Angel. The tiny white Eagles suddenly stopped, as if time stopped, and then they reappeared as white pyramid shaped spaceships. It seemed that all is not what it appears to be!

Later on, I was shown three baby pigeons and a mother pigeon that looked like they were inside my living room. I felt that they were showing me that they were in the area that I live. Right around this time, I was having so many visions of spaceships, that I was beginning to think that I might be abducted!

A month later, my daughter and I decided to go to a psychic fair in Vancouver. While there, I noticed a UFO booth and so I decided to ask if there had been any recent sightings. They told me that there had been a lot of sightings in the last six months. I said "What about recently?" He asked me why I was asking, and I explained to him that I had been having all of these visions of UFO's . The man questioned me as to when I was having the visions. I told him that they began around the end of July (1995) and became the strongest around mid-August. He was quite astonished, and went on to say "Yes, there was a huge sighting, in fact, one of the largest ever reported. The UFO appeared to be 50 feet across and was pyramid shaped. A couple had spotted it three times on the same night.

I asked where and when this had been reported. He said it was spotted on August 12th, and proceeded to give the cross streets, which were exactly where we lived. My daughter was standing behind me, and I could here the gasp come out of her. I had been telling my family about these visions for weeks, but they had just put it off to being strange dreams, or that their mother was losing it! I took out my driver's license and showed him my address. He was quite excited, and asked me what I did for a living. I told him that I was a realtor, but also an artist. He said that for some strange reason most of the people who report these sightings seem to be musicians, writers, or painters. I know that people who are more artistic use the right side of their brain more than the left, and I couldn't help but wonder if we are more intuitive, as well.

Chapter 13

"The Red Rose City"

I was very worried about my son Ryan. I was upset because I had just returned from the emergency room at the local hospital. He had woken up in the middle of the night complaining about his heart pounding again. It was beating so quickly that I could actually see it through his skin, and this had been happening far too often. I had rushed him to the hospital trying to calm him along the way. Once again, they couldn't find anything wrong, and sent us home without any remedy. I had been taking him from doctor to doctor to see if they could find out what was causing these heart palpitations, without success. My son was always complaining about pains in his chest and how tired he was, and this problem with the pounding in his heart not only scared him, but me as well. Rushing him to the emergency room was becoming a regular occurrence. I was very concerned. The doctors had sent him for many tests and couldn't find anything wrong, other than a heart murmur, which they didn't seem concerned about. But they also hadn't prescribed anything to help him, and I was in a state of helplessness.

As I crawled into bed after returning from the hospital, I fell asleep feeling exhausted and very upset. I had the strangest dream. I

91

found myself walking through a long hallway. At the far end I could see a door made of wood with a stained glass window. The wood on the door looked very old, as if it had been there for centuries. I opened the door and found myself standing in front of a vast sandy desert. All of a sudden I was swept away, and it felt as if I was flying until I eventually came to the edge of a mountain cliff. I recall sitting there, and as I looked down I could see the desert area in front of me with some mountains to my left. I noticed a shape, which appeared to be a Pyramid made of pure energy. For some reason, I had the impression that it was "parked" in front of the mountains beside an entranceway or passage that led deep into the mountains. I remember hearing a voice telling me that I would be going through nine gates and that after I passed through the first gate, I would receive a guide, and that my guide's name was Baba. I used to call my grandmother Baba, and I remember thinking to myself, perhaps my husband was right and I am going to die, or have a "near death experience". Maybe my Baba was going to meet me "on the other side" and be my guide.

I suddenly found myself being guided towards the mountain where the opening was. I remember flying through a long passageway, which eventually led me to a courtyard where there was a magnificent temple. It was huge and carved right into the mountain directly facing me. In fact, there appeared to be a whole city carved into the mountains, as well. The temple was quite extraordinary, as it had huge pillars and on the top, sculptures of women in long robes, surrounded by Angels and two lions. I had the impression that this must be a very important place. I couldn't remember anything more about the dream, except that just before I woke up I was shown the words "Air 31". They were typewritten in front of me.

I woke up in the morning wondering what it all meant. It seemed like such a strange dream. I had the feeling that I was really there, and that something more had occurred, but I couldn't remember, or my memory had been blocked, and I wasn't supposed to remember. Of course, I kept wondering what "Air 31" meant. I didn't know much about astrology, but knew that there were such things as "air" signs. I wondered if perhaps something significant was going to occur on the 31st day of an "Air" sign. I tried to find my astrology book, but couldn't seem to find it anywhere. I finally gave up looking for it, and then thought that maybe something special was going to happen to me in 31 days, months, or perhaps even years. I was even trying to figure out how old I would be by then. I was also beginning to wonder if I was hallucinating all of this!

It wasn't until later on that evening, that I began thinking about the dream once again, and suddenly thought that perhaps they were referring to "air waves". Could "Air 31" mean Channel 31? I immediately turned on the TV and found that station. There was a show on, but it was a documentary about police officers and how they have a much greater amount of suicides than other professions, because of their high stress level. I watched the show to see if there was any connection to my dream, but the only similarity I could see was that my son was also going through a lot of stress at the time. He was a goalie on a hockey team, which put a lot of the responsibility of the game onto him. I was hoping that the documentary wasn't showing me that my son was thinking about suicide, because that would be unbearable. I soon realized that this wasn't the show I was supposed to watch, because of what occurred next.

I hadn't really been paying too much attention to the show, and was tidying up a few things when the next program began. I happened to glance up as it started and was absolutely dazed! I could hardly believe it. I'm sure I must have been standing there with my mouth wide open. The documentary began by showing the desert and then the exact same mountains that I had seen in my dream. Suddenly the camera went through this passageway, which apparently was a mile and a half long, and then the camera focused on the most incredible sight. It was the temple I had seen in my dream, and the courtyard where I had seen the words "Air 31". They were showing the city that was built right into the mountains, just like in my dream. Then the title of the documentary was shown: "The Lost City of Petra". Words cannot describe how amazed I was! I called my husband into the room to tell him that I had seen this in my dream the night before. I explained to him that I had even been shown which channel to watch it on. Of course he just laughed and said "Oh, you probably saw it advertised earlier in the week" and that triggered the dream. I thought about what he said, thinking that it was a possibility. But the vision I had seen the night before was so strong, and after what occurred the following day, I was sure that this was not so!

The show was over an hour long and all about this tiny city that was hidden in the desert mountains of Jordan. It was beautifully built, and appeared to be a combination of both Egyptian and Roman styled architecture. It was known as the "Red Rose City" because of the colour of the mountains, which were very red. It is situated between Egypt and Israel, just below the Dead Sea, and was widely used in ancient times as a resting place for travelers. Amazingly, this tiny little desert city had a very complex water system, as well as a Roman style coliseum that seated almost 8,000 people. Petra is now known as one of the new "seven wonders of the world", but at the time that I had this experience, it was not a well-known place. The city had been home to the Nebatean tribe who had once been quite a prominent civilization, but suddenly disappeared (much like the Mayan people). Some people feel that Petra may have been conquered by the Romans, but nobody knows for sure. In the documentary, the Bedouin people expressed strong feelings that this ancient city was haunted, as they would often hear voices at night. Because of this, they were afraid to stay there overnight. Archaeologists had recently found a new area in the city that was tiled and painted with beautiful pictures. Inside they discovered the remains of some burnt documents, which they were in the process of transcribing at the time the documentary was made. The archaeologists had the impression that this was some type of will.

I was really amazed that I was actually shown what channel to watch. I also found it very synchronistic that I was able to figure out "just in time" to watch the show. I wondered about the burnt documents, and why I was guided to watch this documentary. Could it be possible that the "will" had something to do with me? Could it be my own will from a past life? Hmm, what was I supposed to see?

The following day, in the afternoon I began to feel so overwhelmingly tired that I just had to lie down. I had hardly closed my eyes when I instantly I saw my son standing in front of me. He seemed to be standing on a wheel with his hands and feet spread apart. It looked exactly like the drawing of Leonardo DaVinci's - the one known as "the Canon" – showing a man standing on a wheel, except in this vision, DaVinci's man was my son. All of a sudden I felt like I had been pulled right out of my body. It felt like my soul or spirit had left through my "third eye" or the area of the forehead a little above and between the eyes. I saw the words "captured" printed in front of me, and in an instant I was in another place or dimension. I recognized that I was back in the "lost city" once again, standing in front of a long table similar to a picnic table but much larger, and I appeared to be in the courtyard. There was a beautiful young girl who looked about eighteen years old sitting in front of me. She had long wavy black hair and was wearing a headband with a gemstone that was centred right in the middle of her forehead. I remember thinking that she looked like she came from Atlantis, if there was such a place. Her skirt was short, and she was sitting very casually with one leg up on the bench and the other down. In front of her, were a number of small "cone shaped" earthenware pots - which she had been filling with, what I had assumed to be, some type of herbs. When she became aware of my presence, she looked directly at me and said "pure Selenium". I had no idea what Selenium was at the time, as I had never heard of it before. I thought that perhaps she was talking about me, or maybe even calling me that name.

A few moments later, I noticed another woman coming towards me. She had been inside the temple, which was located across from the girl and to my left, but further away. It looked very much like the same temple I had seen the night before. As she came down the stairs, and approached us, I could see her long robes flowing all around her, moving ever so gently as she gracefully took each step. As she came closer to the table, I had the impression that she was really "looking me over". It was as if she was assessing me, and I wasn't sure why. I had the sense that she was seeing whether or not I was "worthy" of something. She looked to be "middle aged" and was incredibly beautiful, dressed like some type of queen or Goddess. Her robe reminded me of a "Roman" styled gown, sleeveless and V-necked, knotted under the breast and made of the most delicate fabric, which fell gently to her feet. While the younger woman appeared to me as "flesh and blood" this gracious being was completely transparent, like a spirit. When the younger girl spoke to me, I could hear her, but when this woman spoke, it was through extra sensory perception, thought transference. The words came into my head "When you receive a gift...." and unfortunately I can't remember the balance of the sentence. Although in my heart, I sensed that I was to do something in return for this gift.

To my right a young man suddenly appeared, dressed in an unusual costume. He was wearing a kilt with sandals that wrapped all the way up to his knees. He wore jewellery wrapped around his upper arms, a headpiece of sorts, and was carrying an unusual looking staff. For some strange reason, I automatically followed this man, as if I subconsciously knew that I was supposed to, and he led me down the stairs into a chamber. I don't remember what happened at that point, but suddenly I discovered myself fully submerged under water and I was looking up. As I floated to the top I could see two carved pillars directly in front and above me. Instantly, I was submerged into the water again (almost like a baptism) – and I don't know how it happened, but suddenly I found myself inside a large rectangular shaped room, and the water had disappeared. The air seemed to be quite normal, and as I looked around, I noticed that the room was quite ornate. The walls were red with some gold ornamentation painted on them, and there were three or four tall stained glass windows, along each of the walls on my left and to my right. The room was filled with the most beautiful veils, that appeared to be ever so gently floating above me, as if some unseen force was holding each of them by a corner and twirling them. They were made of the thinnest and most delicate material, like none I have ever seen and decorated with designs that looked Persian or what you might see on Indian carpets. I stood there hypnotized by their movements, and after a few minutes they gently merged together forming a beautiful canopy that hovered above my head. This was so incredibly beautiful and quite captivating. I wasn't sure what it meant, but I knew that I had just experienced something very special. I wondered if this was "the dance of the seven veils" that one hears about.

Suddenly I found myself back in my room again, and could hear the telephone ringing. I could hardly believe what had happened. I was in a total state of shock! I wondered if it was the phone that brought me back to this "reality". It was a friend of mine. The experience was so vivid and fresh in my mind that I just had to tell someone. I explained to her what had happened and how profound it was. She said that she had also experienced something strange in her life a long time ago, but nothing quite so profound. She emphasized that I should try to find out what Selenium was, or meant. The information I found, said that the word Selenium stemmed from the word "Selene" which means "of the moon" and that it comes from a mineral found in the earth known as Selenite. I was just beginning to learn about gemstones, and had heard that some people believe that specific ones possibly have healing qualities. I called up the local bookstore where I had found the

"Angel" books, as I was aware they also sold crystals, and inquired as to whether they had ever heard of "Selenite" and if they had any. The shop owner mentioned that it actually came in several forms, but he only had one kind in stock, and you can imagine my surprise when he told me it was called "Desert Rose".

.It seemed quite amazing to me that I would find a stone of this name, as the place where I had been taken was known as the "Red Rose City" which is situated in the desert.

This experience was so unusual and profound that I could hardly stop thinking about it. I decided to see if I could find anything more about this place. I looked up Petra in an old encyclopedia, and most of the information was similar to what had been explained on the television show, but at the very end of the article, it said that this place was once believed to be where there was a Temple of Isis. I had never heard that word before, and wasn't sure exactly what "Isis" was or meant, but I discovered that this was the name of an ancient Egyptian Goddess, and sometimes she is referred to as a Moon Goddess. It seemed quite coincidental that the word I had been given "Selenium" also means "of the moon".

During Greek and Roman times, Isis was considered the Universal Mother Goddess, and that she had a great following. She was regarded as the sister and wife of the Egyptian G-d Osiris, whom she had supposedly resurrected from the dead. As well, she was the protector of her son Horus, and because of that, Isis developed special healing skills and was also adept at performing magic. I had the impression that this was the beautiful "spirit" that I had seen coming out of the temple. I couldn't help but wonder if it was possible that she had somehow felt my frustration and concern for my son. Was it possible that she had somehow "captured" my soul, in order to assist me with my son? If so, how amazing was that? Had I broken some type of "time barrier"? I was full of questions!

I decided to visit the bookstore and purchase the piece of "Desert Rose". I was quite impressed when I was shown the gemstone, because it actually looked like little clusters of roses, that are tanned coloured, and appears to be made of compressed sand. I also learned that "Petra" means stone, and this all seemed so synchronistic!

I wasn't sure what to do with the little stone, but it was small enough for my son to put in his pocket, and so I gave it to him, hoping that it would it would somehow help. The next day my friend called me again, very excited. She had been listening to a doctor on a radio talk show, by the name of Dr. Art Hister. He had spent the whole morning talking about "Selenium" and it was something that was supposed to be very good for you, that can be taken internally. I had no idea it was anything like that, so I immediately went to my vitamin "Bible" and looked it up. It stated that Selenium was "a powerful anti-oxidant, good for young boys going through puberty, and especially for their heart and lungs. When I read those words, I could hardly believe it. Of course, since that time, it has become quite well known that Selenium is one of the most powerful anti-oxidents available today, but when I was told about it, I had never heard of it. Another amazing thing I discovered is that the picture of the man standing on a wheel, drawn by Leonardo da Vinci, is a symbol quite commonly used for Vitamins and Minerals! Of course, there are no coincidences!

That afternoon I went to the pharmacy to buy the Selenium. As I went to pay for it, the pharmacist said to me "Oh you must have been listening to Dr. Art Hister this morning." I said "No, I found out about Selenium quite a different way!" After sharing my story with the pharmacist, I could tell by the look on his face that he too was truly amazed. I started giving my son Selenium, and thanks to the Goddess Isis, I didn't have to take him to emergency with heart palpitations anymore.

I can honestly say that nothing quite like this had ever happened to me before. It seemed like I had entered another dimension of time and space! I had been in two places at once, or so it seemed! I wasn't asleep when this first occurred, and so I could hear what was going on in the next room of my house, but was aware that I had left my body in a "catatonic" state at home. I knew that this was probably what had been happening to me when I was sleeping at night, and that some of the visions were "out of body" as well. But this was the first time I had actually been awake when it happened, and you can imagine that this experience was quite remarkable and very profound. It left an impression on me, that I will never forget.

Chapter 14

"Extraordinary People"

The day I went to the bookstore to purchase the "Desert Rose" I decided to see if any new books had come in. I noticed one, in particular, that had some symbols on the cover – similar to those I had seen in some of my dreams. As I stood there gazing at the book, around the corner, on the very bottom shelf, the words "My Baba and I" suddenly caught my eye. Instantly I remembered being told that I was going to go through nine gates, and after passing through the first gate I would meet my guide, whose name was "Baba". I picked up the book and discovered that it was about a man who at that time was living in India, and was an avatar, a spiritual teacher known as Sai Baba, often referred to as just "Baba". I was immediately curious to learn more about this so-called "master" - especially since I thought that he might be my "guide" that I had been told about in the vision.

I discovered that this "being" has some very special qualities that were similar to the ones Jesus was said to have. The book claimed that "Baba" was able to perform miracles, and that many people had even received special gifts from him - that he had literally "pulled out of the air" like gold rings and necklaces. He was also able to manifest something called "vibhutti" which was known as sacred ash. Apparently, the ash would magically appear and was used for healing purposes. I had never heard of anything like this before, and while I wanted to believe that it was possible, I have always been of the opinion that "seeing is believing". While many people claim him to be divine, Baba claims that we are all divine, and that we can also develop these powers.

You can imagine I was quite overwhelmed with this information, and to be quite honest, I had a hard time believing that this could be possible and true.

But a few days later I received a phone call from a friend, and my opinion soon changed. Shirle called to see if I would be interested in going to see a healer that was coming to town. I hadn't been sick or anything, but he was supposedly an interesting speaker, and he would also be giving some workshops. She faxed me a brochure about Geoff Boltwood, who at the time, also called himself "The Source". When I received the fax, I noticed that the first paragraph stated that Geoff Boltwood could manifest rose oil and vibhutti, just as Sai Baba. It seemed very synchronistic that I had only just read about Sai Baba, and here his name was brought to my attention once again. As well, he was able to manifest healing ash, just as Sai Baba. Of course, I wanted to see someone who could actually perform such an amazing feat. The following week, we drove together downtown. The event was held in a Masonic hall on West Broadway in Vancouver, and they charged twenty-two dollars at the door. I didn't realize it at the time, but the number 22 was considered to be a very special number, a master number, and people in the metaphysical community often worked with this number. There must have been at least two or three hundred people gathered in the hall, and once we had settled into our seats, someone made a brief introduction.

Suddenly the doors of the hall burst open, and as Geoff Boltwood entered, the most beautiful scent of roses filled the hall. It was absolutely phenomenal - I had never experienced anything like this ever before. He spoke to us saying that we (humanity) were evolving, and that he was now able to be in two places in the same time, that he was able to "bilocate". As well, he said that some people had seen him become quite transparent, while meditating. Of course, if I hadn't had my own "bilocating to Petra" experience, I probably wouldn't have believed him. He then asked if anybody would like to come up for healing , and my friend Shirle, who had been having problems with her throat, raised her hand, amongst many. He invited her to come onto the stage.

First he had her check his hands and arms to make sure that he wasn't hiding anything up his sleeves. Then he placed his hand on hers and pressed down. The oil appeared in the palm of her hand. Geoff asked her to take it back to her seat and share it with the people around her. She was ecstatic. On the way home she mentioned that her throat was actually feeling much better!

I was told that this amazing man was going to be here for about 3 or 4 more days and would be holding seminars. I would have loved to have taken one of his courses, but they were way out of my price range, but even more, I would have loved to have had the opportunity to see "up close" the manifestation of the sacred oil. "When the student is ready, the teacher appears." I learned that if you ask for something that will serve a higher purpose, it can and will happen.

The very next day, I received a phone call from my friend telling me that Geoff would be having a small audience in his hotel room with only ten people, and it would cost only $33.00 (another master number). I could hardly believe my good fortune. It was almost unbelievable, that out of three hundred people, I was being given the opportunity to be one of those ten, and that I could afford it!

As we drove up, a parking spot appeared right in front of the building, a rare occurrence in the west end of downtown Vancouver. We lived the furthest away, and so we were the last to arrive. When we went upstairs, we were told that the group had been mentally creating a parking space for us, so that they could begin right away. They certainly did a good job!

After a short meditation, Geoff came into the room, and I was very excited when he invited me to be the first one to receive this sacred essence. Again, he let me see that he had nothing up his sleeves or in his hands, then he placed his hand face down, on mine. There in the palm of my hand appeared a little pool of oil, which had the most beautiful scent of Roses! I was truly overwhelmed.

Geoff asked me if there was anything I needed healed or if I had any questions. I said my pelvic area had been hurting lately, and also that I was looking for work. I had put my real estate license on hold because the market had dropped drastically. He asked me what it was, that I wanted to do, but I said I really hadn't thought about it. Although, secretly, I truly wished to be able to do what he was doing, spreading God's fragrances!

Before we left, we mingled a bit with some of the other people. One of the ladies there was a channel for "Archangel Michael". I told her about the phenomenal visions that I had been experiencing, and also about my "wake up call" from Archangel Ariel. She told me that a lot of people were channeling Ariel at that time! It somehow felt comforting to know that, I was not alone.

On my way home my body began to feel strange from the waist to the thighs. The only way I can describe it, would be to say that it felt like pins and needles all over. After about half an hour it went away, and I noticed that the pain I had been experiencing was gone, but the experience had been a little frightening.

Within a month my sister called to say someone she knew needed a salesperson immediately, and I would be paid quite well. It would be demonstrating fragrances in department stores! So there I was "spreading Gods fragrances. Of course, I would have preferred doing it Geoff's way, but I definitely had my wish answered!

A few weeks later, I found myself in a store at the other end of the city, quite far from where I lived. There were hardly any customers, and my co-workers and I were quite bored standing around. I began talking to one of the other women I was working with, Kami, who mentioned that she had recently returned from India. Upon questioning her about it, she went on to say that she felt quite blessed, because while she was there, she had the opportunity to meet two of the most amazing people in the world. She had met Mother Teresa, and had been invited by her to spend several days assisting her. It was only a few years later that Mother Teresa died. Kami is the only person I know who had the opportunity to personally meet this wonderful woman who devoted her whole life to nurturing others. Then Kami mentioned that she had also met an avatar by the name of Sai Baba. I was shocked. Once again, I had only heard about this avatar just weeks before, when suddenly I met someone that had actually met him!

Of course, I asked Kami if she had seen him perform any miracles. She explained that he was mingling through the crowd and acknowledged her with his eyes. He bowed to her, threw both arms towards her and a bouquet of Roses appeared out of thin air, which she caught. Although this was quite an amazing feat, Kami made a point of explaining to me that she was more impressed with her experience helping Mother Teresa, than witnessing this manifestation. Of course, I have the greatest respect for Mother Teresa, but I was still in a state of shock about the synchronicities around Sai Baba, and I had been impressed by the fact that he could perform such miracles. I told her about my dream and that Baba was supposed to be my guide. Kami seemed to be more impressed with "my experience" than having roses thrown to her by an avatar! I was also beginning to notice that roses seemed to be appearing everywhere!

The next day Kami told me that she had been invited to sing at a Bajan, which I learned was the Hindu word for a gathering of people to sing spiritual prayers. The Bajan was for Sai Baba, and she invited me to attend. I asked if I could bring a friend, and she said that all were welcome.

Chapter 15

"Soul Sisters"

I had met my friend Val shortly after I began having the visions. I had picked up a small newsletter while in the metaphysical store, and there were several "messages" written by various authors. I noticed one author that I particularly resonated with.

I noticed an ad for a meditation, and decided to call the phone number listed. I spoke to the woman, and shared a few of my experiences with her. After awhile, she mentioned that she had a friend that she would really like me to meet, a woman who lived in the same area as I did. She believed that we had a lot in common. She gave me Val's number, and at the same time mentioned that she was also the author of some of the articles written in the newsletter. It turned out to be the same person whose "messages" I had been drawn to. I was quite hesitant about calling her at first, because I truly believed that someone with her knowledge, would be much too busy to be bothered with someone like myself. I envisioned line-ups of people waiting to meet this amazing woman, but eventually I did get enough nerve to make the phone call.

Val was so incredibly friendly, and she wanted to meet for coffee right away. I finally had a chance to talk to someone about the visions, and Val was happy to have met me, as well. She explained that everyone else she knew seemed to be having a very different type of experience. She was also having visions about Angels, Eagles and Spaceships! I immediately felt very close to Val, and although she was several years younger than me, I felt that her soul was much older than mine. She became my teacher.

Val believes that the earth is populated with souls from other planets and universes, and that she and I most likely came from the same place, or perhaps were soul sisters. She also believed that we belonged to the Order of Melchizadek. (Mel –kee-za-dek)

I had learned about someone of that name when I was researching the stories in the "Old Testatment" for my Art show. Melchizadek had been mentioned in the story of Abraham. He had appeared to Abraham, claiming to be a "Priest of G-d of the Highest" and was without father or mother, or even genealogy. I wondered if that Melzhizadek had any connection to the "Order" that Val was talking about.

Val explained that this was a Divine Order, which exists among all the planets of the solar system. She explained that it was an Order that Angels also belonged to. I remember thinking that it seemed hard to believe that I could belong to something so special. She said that this "order" was also a Mystery School and that its' initiates are scattered throughout the universe as well as around the earth. It even has its' own qualifications and requirements for admission. Its main purpose: to help bring about "enlightenment" through its incarnated initiates. Val explained that many people belong to this Order, even though they may not be aware of it. If you are reading this, it could be possible that you too, are a member of this Divine Order.

Val also spoke to me about "leylines" and "energy" to me. I had previously learned about leylines in one of the books I had read, but, she explained it a little differently. She said that the earth has certain areas which have higher amounts of energy than other areas. She said that many Churches and Temples were built on these leylines, and that because many prayers have been said for thousands of years in these places, the energy is pure and sacred. The energy can also be found in pristine natural surroundings, like the desert, old forests, waterfalls, and lakes of pure water.

She went on to explain that when we visit these places, our own energy fields pick up the surrounding energy, which then becomes part of our being. Therefore, the more sacred places we visit, the more information we carry in our energy field. When we meet other people, there is an exchange of information on a "soul level". This seemed very amazing to me. I thought about all of the different places that I had visited when I had been traveling in Europe and the Middle East, many years prior. If what she was telling me was true, then I must be carrying around a lot of "information". I wondered if that had anything to do with the visions and dreams.

It was Val who introduced me to crystals, and through her, I had the opportunity to meet some very interesting people, and I began collecting and learning about the healing and channeling aspects of stones. I really became enthralled with them and my collection grew rapidly. Not only are crystals beautiful to look at, but they each have their own unique qualities and purpose. I found a book called the "Woman's Book of Healing" by Dianne Stein, which had a lot of information about healing, as well as information about working with crystals.

Val also said that Sai Baba had come to her several times while she was meditating. She said that she felt so much joy when he came around, and was really surprised when she learned that this person actually lived on the planet! She told me that Sai Baba embodied the energy of Love at a cosmic level and that His work, in part, was to prepare humanity for the work of the Christ, by awakening the love principle in humanity. Val also told me that there was a controversy about this avatar, that some people believed that he was the "Cosmic Christ" but that others thought that he shouldn't have been using his powers for manifesting things like jewelry. As well, there were some that felt that he was a fake. What bothered her the most, was that some people were worshipping him, which many people, believed to be wrong. I too felt that this was wrong, as I have always believed that we should only worship God. In his book Baba tells people not to worship him, and that each of us are divine, as well. Val said that the feeling that she had when he appeared in her meditations, was that he was "an embodiment of love".

I called Val and asked her if she would like to accompany me to a "Bajan" for Sai Baba. She said that she would, and so the two of us went together. It turned out that the gathering was in Surrey, British Columbia, a suburb of Vancouver, and not too far from where Val and I lived. In fact our homes created a perfect triangle. The Bajan was in a woman's home, and there must have been around a hundred people there, including Kami and her husband, who were singing. The singing lasted for about an hour, and the highlight of the evening, for us, was when they passed around the sacred healing ash known as "Vibhutti". Val and I were asked to share our personal experiences relating to Sai Baba, which we did. Afterwards, they served a huge feast of Indian food, and we had an opportunity to meet some of the people. There was one man that was wearing a ring that Baba had manifested especially for him, and he was very proud of it.

While Val and I were the only Caucasian people there, it turned out that the hostess had also been having many visions, similar to ours, and we soon realized that we had met another "soul sister". Her name was Kamal, which means Lotus Blossom, and she made us stay after everyone else had left. We talked until about 3:00 in the morning, sharing our personal experiences. We became very good friends, and would meet regularly for some interesting discussions, and we also went to many metaphysical events together over the years.

The night I went home from the Bajan, I had another strange dream. Some spaceships had landed, and there seemed to be some type of an emergency or tragedy that was happening, but I seemed to be quite calm and collected. The people in the dream were arriving to help us so that we could lead the people to the ships. They looked human, and they were dressed in white satin robes, which had large hoods trimmed in gold, that were draped around their heads. I felt that they were men and women of God.

Mysteriously, a few months later, my sister picked up an art card in a garage sale and gave it to me. It was an Indian woman playing a sitar, dressed in a white satin robe with a hood embroidered in gold. Behind her were what appeared to be huge starships in the sky, and there were flames in the streets. It seemed that someone else had painted my vision, except that they put Kamal in the painting. I had the dream the same night I had met her playing the sitar.

Shortly after, I was offered a position with a cosmetic company as a promotional assistant. I would work in department stores as a "make-up artist" and "skin care consultant". As well, during promotional events, I would give free gifts to customers with each of their purchases. I have to say, I was feeling a bit guilty about selling the cosmetics at such high prices. I mentioned this to Kamal and she said "Why don't you ask Baba what he thinks?" That night I asked the question before I fell asleep. I had a dream in which I was selling cosmetics for Baba and as I handed someone a bag, I said "...... you get a free gift *and* Vibhutti". I called Kamal in the morning to tell her about the dream . She laughed and said "Baba is showing you that you are giving them a type of healing when you give them a "makeover" or "skin care" treatment!

Chapter 16

"Mount Sinai"

Val, Kamal and I were attending some metaphysical events on Friday evenings. There was a Masonic Hall in the area that would have some very interesting people come to speak. The three of us would attend these lectures and then go for coffee later to discuss what transpired during the evening. While some of it was boring, most of it was extremely interesting and for me, very educational. It was almost like taking a course on metaphysics.

On one of those evenings, we met a woman who had the most interesting story to tell. Her name was Christa Burka. We had been told that this particular evening was going to be about crystals, and so we expected to see some on display, and learn about them. Instead, this turned out to be one of the most interesting evenings, as we listened to the fascinating story this woman had to tell.

While vacationing in Hawaii, Christa had been planning on taking a course on healing. In the morning, while meditating, she received a message telling her not to take the course, that she had another calling. She was told that she was going to write a book about crystals and that she would be receiving hers very shortly. Of course this surprised her, as she knew nothing about crystals. In fact, the only kind of crystals she knew about were the ones you "drink out of". Later that afternoon she heard a knock on her door and upon opening it, she discovered that a large box had been left at her door.

You can imagine her shock after opening it, to find a "crystal" along with a note from a friend. In the note, her friend explained that after Christa left for Hawaii, he had decided to take a trip to Israel. While there, he had an opportunity to visit Mount Sinai and climb the mountain where Moses had supposedly received the "Ten Commandments". Just as he reached the forty-fourth step, a Bedouin jumped out and handed him two crystals, saying that one was for him and the other was "for a friend". The Bedouin said "You will know who it is for." Christa's friend *knew* that the crystal was meant for her. Of course there was a lot more to the story. But I found it very odd that this happened on Mount Sinai

While doing my research for the art show, I recalled that gemstones had been specified by G-d to be placed on the "breastplate" of Aaron, Moses' brother, who became the first High Priest of Israel. When Moses had been given the Commandments on Mount Sinai, he had also been instructed how the garment of the High Priest was to be made, which included a special breastplate. It was to have twelve stones embedded into it, in a specific pattern of three columns of four stones. These represented the twelve tribes of Israel. The breastplate also had two special objects hidden inside, possibly stones or pebbles, known as "Urim" and "Thummim" which were used by the High Priest as oracles. I was surprised to learn that the Hebrew people believed in oracles.

I had included a painting called "The Diamond Cutters" in my art show. I had discovered that most of the people who belonged to this profession were "orthodox" (very religious) Jews. I had wondered about this, and learned that because this type of industry dealt with Diamonds and other valuable stones, these people had to have very high ethics, people that could be trusted with such vast amounts of wealth. I couldn't help but wonder if perhaps these people have known about the power of crystals for centuries and kept it a well-guarded secret. If so, why? If the stones were able to help people to heal, then this knowledge should have been shared. Then I remembered what Val had told me. She said that during the time of Atlantis, the crystals had been used for many things, both good and bad. They had learned how to unlock their power and unfortunately, it was through the wrongful use of crystals that Atlantis came to her fall.

After listening to Christa's story, I thought about the time I had been to Mount Sinai. In March of 1973, I had been visiting and traveling around Israel for about six months. A group of us decided to rent a Jeep and drive through the desert. I found it fascinating. It seemed amazing to me, that little children were actually living and playing right in the middle of the desert. These were the Bedouin children, and they were so cute! They were all dressed in faded beige sackcloth dresses. They looked at us curiously with their huge dark brown eyes lined in kohl, the traditional black powder used to protect their eyes from the sun, and cosmetically enhance their eyes. All of the children had smiling faces and tiny bare feet. As we passed through the small villages, we could see women dressed completely in black, from head to toe, with veils covering their faces. They were just sitting in the hot sun like statues. Flies would be attracted to them and even land on them, but they would just sit there in a meditative state as if they hadn't even noticed. Eventually we stopped at one small site where we found a little supply hut. They sold wheat, beans and other dry goods, and of course Coca-cola! I was really amused at that! Right in the middle of the desert!

As we traveled on, we stopped to pick up a Bedouin wanderer, who just seemed to appear out of nowhere. This man was incredibly handsome. He had dark flashing eyes, like Omar Sharif, and was also dressed in long black robes, with a turban on his head. I found it a bit odd to find someone traveling by foot all alone in the middle of the desert. There didn't seem to be anyone or anything around. He was just standing there, all alone. We gave him a lift, and as we sat there in the jeep, I recall feeling that there was something special about this man, he had a wonderful essence about him. I have often wondered about him throughout the years. He asked us to stop at a specific place, which turned out to be a beautiful oasis, where he led us to a natural well hidden amongst several palm trees. It was one of the most beautiful places I have ever seen. He gave each of us a drink, and you can imagine how wonderful it was to taste such pristine water, after traveling in the heat of the desert for several hours. We left the man there and continued our journey.

Eventually I came upon some information about someone called "Matreya". I was told that he was the person, who some people believe to be the messiah. I was shown a photograph of this man, who apparently just appears out of nowhere. I was surprised when I saw the photo, because he reminded me so much of the man who we had given a lift to in the desert. At first I thought that it was just a coincidence that he looked so similar. I didn't believe that it could possibly be the same person, until I read the following: "Maitreya goes all over the world creating healing waters. The most important thing is that a network is being created throughout the world, energetically linked together; a network of "the Waters of Life". These flow on the physical plane through wells and water sources, and on the emotional-astral planes, as well as the mental and spiritual planes.

In the article, someone asked if there was a quicker way to find these healing waters created by Maitreya, and the answer was "No. The water is discovered in a definite, lawful rotation. Maitreya brings about the finding. The waters appear to be found by chance, but someone is always impressed to find the water."

I was truly shocked to read the last part, as the man we met, brought us to the water, and we were definitely impressed when he took us there. I haven't been in touch with any of the other people who were with me at that time, but I can't help but wonder if they are also having some type of spiritual awakening. This happened in 1973.

Finally we reached our destination. We had been told previously, before we left Eilat (the place where we had rented the jeep) not to camp out. We had been warned that it would be wiser if we stayed at the army base close by, because the Bedouins couldn't be trusted and we could possibly get stabbed in the back. Well, if I haven't already mentioned this, I have never been one to follow rules. Four of us decided to find a place to camp and the other four stayed at the army baracks. We began searching for a place to camp out.

At the base of Mount Sinai, there is a Monastery known as St. Catharine's, which is enclosed within a wall. Beside the monastery, we found another small building, which also had a wall around it. We thought that perhaps this was the original temple. We began to investigate the area, and after entering, we discovered that the building was closed, so we went around to the back of the temple to see if there was some place where we could camp for the night. This was where we found a very tiny mud hut with some Bedouin living there. There was a woman who was the same age as me, which was 25 at the time. She too, was dressed totally in black and she had her hair braided into the shape of a cone, which protruded from the top of her forehead, like a unicorn! She wore a black headpiece and a veil of golden coins. Her eyes were fascinating, large, and outlined in Kohl, dark and very intriguing.

I learned later that the men and women of the desert wear many layers of clothing beneath an outer layer of black. As it gets hot throughout the day, the black layer attracts the heat causing them to perspire. The moisture soaks into the layers closest to the skin and then the damp clothing acts as a cooling agent for the rest of the day.

We also noticed a younger girl, whom we asked about. It turned out that she was only thirteen years old. She was extremely shy, and would only stand at the doorway of the little hut, peeking out at us. I was surprised to learn that she was also a wife to the same man that the 25 year old woman was married to. I asked the woman where her husband was, and she said that he was away. (I wondered if he had been the handsome man we had encountered earlier.) The Bedouin people travel throughout the desert trading their wares with each other. There was an older man staying with them, which we thought was her father, or father-in-law. He looked to be very old, as he was very wrinkled and extremely tiny, but had a twinkle in his eye.

We sat on the ground around a campfire the whole evening and tried to carry on a conversation with them. Even though none of us spoke the same language, we still managed to communicate, and I truly experienced one of the most fascinating evenings of my life. These people hardly had anything to eat, yet they shared what little they had. They baked some pita bread on a fire, which we ate with enthusiasm. Of course, we shared whatever we had brought to eat with them, which was mostly oranges.

We were supposed to get up at 4:00 AM to go climb the mountain, to see where Moses was given the ten commandments, but we had been up all night, and slept right through to the morning. It was too late to climb the mountain, as you have to be down before the sun gets too hot, as it is in the desert. We were all so excited about camping out with the Bedouin, that we didn't care, as we felt that our experience was also very exciting and unique.

I remember telling this story to a friend one time, and she stated that this woman must have felt like we were aliens from another world. It's ironic that we brought "oranges" as did my visitor from another dimension. We felt that oranges were the perfect fruit to travel with. They have a natural covering, therefore you don't have to worry about germs. They quench your thirst, while filling your stomach, and you can share them without the need for a knife.

For many years, ever since I had my experience with the orange, I have wondered if they had a special significance. I had noticed that Buddhists, Sikhs and Hindu people put oranges on their alters as offerings, and Jewish people give out oranges at Purim and

Hannukah. Its meaning was finally revealed to me in a message that came through in the middle of the night on April 11th 2009. It was part of a poem: *"the gift you received is the "light of the world" from the Orange, that was illuminated and glowing, for enlightenment has flowed from the "ones of old" as the petals of love were unfolding".*

Chapter 17

"Ancient Jewish Mysticism"

September, 1995 – I was asleep, yet felt as if someone had awakened me once again. Flaming golden letters began streaming into the middle of my forehead, right in the area known as the "third eye". It was a very strange experience, yet while this was happening, I had the most wonderful feeling come over me. It was as if each flame held an essence of pure love. I immediately recognized the letters as being Hebrew, as I had studied the Aleph-Bet as a child, but these were coming so quickly, that I wasn't able to identify any of them. I remember thinking to myself "This is great, God's talking to me, and I can't understand Him!"   I decided that if it happened again, I would try to remember at least one letter, but knew that I would have to find some type of reference book to find out which letters they were.   Then I began seeing geometrical shapes, which came in a kaleidoscope of colours. They also were pulsing into my "third eye".   I was off to the book store once again, searching for the answers, and came across a book called "Words of Power" by Brian and Esther Crowley, which helped greatly. I learned that each letter of the Hebrew alphabet has a specific meaning. They are also associated with a number, as well.   I discovered that the Hebrew

Flaming Letters is a "Language of Light" and in Hebrew the experience is called "Kaballah" which means "to receive".

Kabbalah, which seems to be spelled many different ways (Cabala, Quaballa, Kaballa, etc.) is a form of "Ancient Jewish Mysticism". From what I read, you had to be at least forty years old, and have a thorough understanding of the Hebrew Old Testament (Torah) before you are allowed to study it. Not only that, it was a secret teaching that only men were allowed to study. I am a woman and the only biblical knowledge that I have is from the stories I learned as a child, and the ones I had read more recently while preparing for my art show. To my knowledge, the only part I had "fulfilled" was that I was over forty!

Even though I had never really been interested in my own religion before, I wondered why I was the one to receive this, although I have to admit, it all seemed very exciting. I shared some of the experiences with a relative, who told me that from what he had heard, Kabbalah was about having a "relationship with God, but in a more personal way". He didn't really know much more about it, as he wasn't religious either. Of course I was intrigued at this point, and wanted to find out more.

I discovered that this was an Angelic teaching created by G-d to answer questions about the nature of the Universe, and the destiny of mankind. It was also created to awaken the mind and all the hidden knowledge inside of man. Well, it certainly did wake up my mind, now all I had to do was find the knowledge. I wondered if the Egyptian symbols, the Angelic visits, and the "space ships" had anything to do with Kabbalah.

There are two different stories regarding how "Kaballah" came into existence. According to ancient tradition, it was a "Secret Doctrine" that was originally taught by G-d to a group of Angels, who had formed a school in Heaven. But, after Adam's fall, the Angels passed on the teaching to mankind in order to help humanity regain the grace of God.

The other story is that the biblical person Abraham, whose name was originally Abram, received Kabbalah directly from G-d when he was about to sacrifice his child. I am not sure if the stories of the Bible are true or not, but I found it very disturbing that G-d would ask that of anyone. I don't think I would have the courage to do anything like that, and would rather give myself, than one of my children. It seemed very cruel to me, but it seems that "sacrifice" was something very common amongst many of the ancient traditions. It is well known that the Mayan and Peruvian people also sacrificed their children. In the story of Abraham, it appears that he was being tested for his belief in God, and was asked to bring his son Isaac as an "offering". Following God's wishes, he was about to place Isaac on the Alter, when suddenly a Ram appeared in the bushes. It was then that G-d spoke to him, telling him NOT to sacrifice his son, but to take the Ram's life instead. It is believed that Abraham received Kaballah at that time, and he was also told the Holy Name of God.

The Hebrew letters "Yod Hey Vov Hey" make up the name, and its meaning in English is "I Am That I AM". In the "Words of Power" book, they said that if one says those words it is one of the highest prayers we can say. The Hebrew name was considered to be so sacred and powerful that the correct pronunciation was kept secret, and forbidden to be used, in case it got might get into the wrong hands. In fact, whenever the name was written in the Torah, other words were substituted, like "Adonai" or "Elohim". Apparently Elohim implies pluralism, which gives one the impression that G-d was sometimes referred to as more than one being, and I couldn't help wonder if this was true. Only the priests of the Temple were allowed to learn the correct pronunciation of the Sacred Name, and the few times it was used, was during prayers on the holiest days of the year.

But even though the Rabbis tried to keep it a secret, the name became known amongst a few mystics during the Middle Ages, and they used it to heal the sick and banish evil spirits. They became known as "Masters of the Name". The Kaballists believe that each of us have a Divine spark of God's essence within us. I also learned that this teaching honours all people, of all belief systems.

The secret teaching was verbally handed down through the generations - first to Abraham's son Isaac, and then to Jacob, who passed it down to his favorite son, Joseph, who was famous for his "coat of many colours". In the story of Joseph, his brothers sold him into slavery, because they thought their father favoured him.

He was taken to Egypt and somehow ended up in prison. It was while there, that Joseph gained a reputation for interpreting dreams. At the time, the Egyptian people believed that those who had this gift, were very special, and highly respected. They also got paid very well. Pharoah was having some very strange dreams around that time, and upon hearing about Joseph, he summoned him to have his dreams interpreted. Pharoah was so pleased with what Joseph told him, that he rewarded him with his freedom and gave him an important position in Egypt. It was through this high office that Joseph was able to eventually bring his father into Egypt. Then Joseph and his father, Jacob, were able to secretly pass on their teachings of their belief in "One God" to the Hebrew people that were living in Egypt. But the "Secret Doctrine" appeared to become lost, or at least hidden, never to be heard of again until the time of Moses.

When Ramses II came into power, he heard a rumour that a King would be born among the Hebrew people. Threatened by this, he demanded that all newly born sons be cast into the Nile. It was during this time that Moses was born and his mother, concerned for his life, had his sister, Miriam, hide the baby amongst the bulrushes. Eventually he was discovered by one of the King's wives, who adopted him, and raised him as one of Pharoah's sons. Moses' real mother managed to get a job as a nursemaid for him, allowing her to carry on a relationship with her him, yet saving him from being sacrificed by Pharoah.

Moses was raised knowing about his Hebrew background, but also became very adept in the Egyptian religion. When he grew up, he saw how badly the Pharoah treated the Hebrew people, and in a fit of anger, killed one of the cruel overseers. It was at this point that Moses fled into the desert, never to be seen for many years. Eventually he met a woman and was married, living many years in the desert.

He was actually quite elderly when G-d spoke to him through a burning bush, asking him to return to Egypt, to plead with Pharoah to let his people go. He was told by G-d to meet with his brother Aaron, and together they would lead the Hebrew people out of Egypt, which they did. After escaping from Egypt, many miracles happened to keep them alive. The Red Sea parted for them, allowing them to cross, and food fell from the sky to feed them. They followed a "cloud by day" and "pillar of fire" by night. They wandered through the desert for forty years, until Moses returned to the mountain where he spoke to G-d through the burning bush once again. It was at this time that Moses received the "Commandments" and the "Secret Doctrine of Kaballah". This was the very same mountain where I had spent the night with the Bedouins. If the story was true, it all seemed very amazing.

I found it strange that the Rabbis of today, are not allowed to study Kaballah until they are over the age of forty. I wondered if it was because Moses had wandered through the desert for over forty years. Could that be a metaphor for wandering aimlessly through life without direction until forty? After all, it is around that time than men go through "mid-life crises" and women become menopausal. Is that the time they begin to ask those questions about their existence? Who am I, what am I, and why am I here? They begin to wonder what their purpose is. I was especially upset when I learned that women weren't allowed to study the mystical teachings!

So the knowledge was lost, or perhaps hidden, after Joseph went into Egypt, but was revealed once again, when Moses came out of Egypt. I can understand G-d sending the "Secret Knowledge" to Abraham and Moses, but why would He be sending it to me? I am truly in awe and grateful for having these experiences, but I don't think I quite fit into the picture. These people were very important biblical figures, but I haven't done anything to feel worthy of such knowledge, besides, it sounds like this might come with some great responsibility! Maybe there was some type of mistake, perhaps this should have been sent to Oprah, or some other person, who has a huge audience, but surely, not me! Not that I'm doubting God. After all that has happened, I surely don't doubt His existence.

After Moses received the stone tablets, a special Ark was built to specifications, covered in gold, and Angels were carved and placed on the lid of the box, with their wings facing each other. The commandments were placed in side the box, along with a menorah (candle holder). The Ark is the famous "lost" one, which many books and movies have been written about, and the information on the tablets became what is known as the Torah, or Old Testament.

The Ark was carried around by the Hebrew people from place to place, until finally David brought it into the temple that was built by his son Solomon, who was King. The Temple was built especially for the Ark, and it was placed inside what was known as the "Holy of Holies". Eventually the Temple was destroyed, and the Ark was stolen. I remember reading about the Ark when I was preparing for my art show. I chose it to be the subject matter for one of my paintings. Interestingly, I changed my mind and painted over it with lotus blossoms, which are one of the symbols of enlightenment. On looking back, the whole exercise seems quite metaphoric. Perhaps one needs to become enlightened in order to find the "Lost Ark".

Apparently Moses only shared the "Secret Knowledge" with seventy of the tribe's elders, which was passed on "orally" through the generations, but only to very few. Eventually it was written down in a book called the Sepher Yetsirah (the Book of Formation) by Rabbi Akiba, sometime between 500 BC and 500 AD. Only ten pages long, the book states that G-d created the Universe through the Hebrew Alphabet, which is comprised of twenty-two letters, and ten numbers. These are called paths and symbolize all of the ideas that relate to the universe. I believe that these were the Hebrew Flaming Letters that I experienced. Kaballah teaches that G-d is pure everlasting energy that fills the Universe. It is believed by Kaballists that the Hebrew letters that form the Name "Yod Hey Vov Hey" actually form the blueprint for the entire Universe, and represent the Human Body, the original form known as the Adom Kadmon.

Chapter 18

"The Zohar"

"I found myself walking along a beautiful beach. I could see a huge rainbow that filled the whole sky. At the upper left of the rainbow was the most beautiful pure White Eagle soaring around. On the following night, I found myself sitting on the beach once again, the sky was totally clear and it appeared to be early evening. The White Eagle had landed on the beach, and was walking towards me. He let me pet his head and his wing, and I recall thinking how large he was and how soft his feathers felt. On the third evening, I found myself flying on the back of the White Eagle. I could see the earth below and slightly behind me, we were flying toward the light".

About a year later, I had the opportunity to talk to a Rabbi. I shared this sequence of dreams with him. He said that he found it interesting that I had mentioned this, because it is written in the Torah, that "we will return to G-d on the wings of an Eagle." I was quite surprised, as I didn't know the Torah said anything about Eagles. I wondered if the Torah said anything about spaceships.

Sometime later, I had an unusual thing happen in the middle of the night. It felt like someone was pouring perfume into my "third eye".

It was a clear liquid essence, and it came in a "feminine shaped" bottle. In fact it looked exactly like a perfume called "Pleasures". As the liquid was being poured, I felt the most wonderful sensation throughout my body, and I have to say it definitely was "pleasurable". I don't remember seeing anyone at the time, but I heard a voice telling me that this was "the Zohar".

Of course, upon waking, I wondered what this meant, and upon looking it up, discovered that this, too, is part of Kaballah, and supposedly the most sacred part of the teaching. In English it is referred to as the "Book of Brightness" or "Book of Splendor". I found it interesting that they chose a perfume called "Pleasures" to represent "Splendor". How clever!

A few nights later, I had the most profound experience. I would have to say it was more like a vision than a dream, and even though it was something that one would not experience on this dimension, it felt very real. I was taken to see a beautiful elderly man. He had the most serene and loving look on his face, with a gentleness that was indescribable. He was wearing a light blue robe, and was seated. As he leaned forward, his pure white hair looked so soft and fell gently to the ground. He had a staff in his right hand that looked like a shepherd's hook, and he was seated on a stone with a symbol carved onto it. This looked like the number three with a written letter "s" beside it. I found out later that this is a Hindu symbol for peace and is called "Om". I learned that this sound can be used, and the symbol gazed upon during meditation in order to reach a higher level of consciousness.

This man did not look like a spirit to me, but flesh and blood. As I gazed at this spectacular vision, I was surrounded in flames, and behind the seated man, were what appeared to be the tablets with the "commandments" that were given to Moses. The "stones" were being held by several baby angels, known as cherubs, flying behind this gentle "being". Below the tablets, was a word written in Hebrew Flaming Letters. I didn't know the meaning of the word, but one of the letters, which looked very similar to a "y" in English, was rising out of the word, and I felt that it must have had some special meaning. Below this word was the Christian symbol of a fish, with the bones inside it. Words cannot describe how I felt when I had this vision.

I thought "this must be Moses" as I stood there mesmerized by this "being". Then I became aware that there was a White Eagle hovering above my left shoulder, and an Eye above this man. The Eye was alive and it too was made of flames, as was the symbol of the hand that floated above the shepherd's hook, held in the right hand of the man, who was facing me. The hand looked like the "Hamsa" charm that I had been shown before, which is used for protection by the people of the Middle East.

Directly behind this gracious soul, and above the tablets, there was a "Being of Light". Rays of exceptionally bright light were beaming from his body, in every direction and he was surrounded in violet and golden flames. Across his chest was a sword with some Hebrew writing on it. I later realized that this must have been Michael, the Archangel. It seemed that I was being shown symbols from several different religions that were connected to these "Beings". This was truly a profound experience! As the flames surrounded me, I felt that I was submerged in the feeling of "Love". I never for a moment thought that I would be allowed to see God, but I felt that I was truly in the presence of someone very special. The following night I was taken to a different place. I remember passing by this same gentle being, and asked who he was. I was told "Abraham".

I looked up the letter I had seen rising out of the others. I would have loved to been able to remember what the whole word looked like, but I was so overwhelmed by the whole experience, that I was lucky to even remember one letter! It turned out to be the Hebrew letter "Ayin" and the meaning was quite amazing. It is the sixteenth letter of the Hebrew alphabet, and represents the number 70. The rest of the interpretation confirmed my experience: The letter "Ayin" means "eye" or "source" and the spiritual light of God. According to Hebrew teachings, this divine light is far greater than the light that emanates from the sun and stars. Though concealed in the Torah (the Old Testament) the "spiritual" eye can behold the presence of this radiance, but only by means of inner eye given by the Ruach HaKodesh (Holy Spirit). The meaning of this one letter was truly the expression of what I had seen. I felt truly blessed.

Ayin

I had also been given the words "A bra man". This happened a few days before the vision and I remember it well, because I kept repeating it over and over in order to remember it, as it seemed like it was something important that they were trying to tell me. They showed me a "bra" so that I would remember it. In the morning I looked up the word and the only word I could find similar was Brahman. This is the name of someone who has reached the highest level of Hinduism. They are considered to be A Brahman, a God-Man. I know that Abraham is the father of the Jewish people, as well as the Christians and Arabs, but is He also connected to Hinduism as well? I couldn't help but wonder.

I was able to remember so many details about the visions, but amazingly, I was never able to remember who the "being" was that was taking me to these places. Before we passed Abraham, we stopped at a place along the way where my father and my stepfather came out to see me. They were both passed away, and seemed to be at the seventh level, one of the levels I was passing through. They both hugged me and told me that I was doing a good job. I wasn't sure what they meant by that! I vaguely remember that the "being" I was with was holding my hand, but was carrying a small baby lamb under their other arm. Eventually we came to a "Being" who was so large that all I can remember seeing were the feet, and my head was somewhere around the hemline of His or Her robe. When I shared this experience with my friend Val, she asked me who I thought it was. I said "Metatron". I just blurted out the name, and I don't know where it came from, because I really had no idea who or what Metatron was. I later discovered that this is the name of an Archangel, and he is the tallest and most powerful of all the Angels. Metatron occupies the throne next to God.

In 1999, I came across a book called "Z-5, The Secret Teachings of the Golden Dawn by Pat Zalewski. In the book there was a passage that suggested that the Story of Abraham represents the awakening of the human soul to the recognition of a Divine Presence, which is followed by a sacrifice. I felt that this described what I had experienced.

I had been "Awakened" by the Angel Ariel, and the vision of Abraham had made me feel that I was surrounded or in the presence of someone Divine. When I had been taken to see Metatron the following night, a lamb had been brought with us. Although I didn't recall seeing it sacrificed, I wondered if this was what happened, and I couldn't help but wonder if it had been sacrificed instead of me.

I wanted to know more about the Zohar, and I discovered some *very* interesting facts. The most interesting was that G-d was also a woman! This I felt was too good to be true. Apparently, the Zohar explains that there is a "female aspect of God" and She is known as the "Shekinah". I found this amazing, because even though I am Jewish, I had never been taught or even heard that the Jewish people acknowledged there was a female aspect of God. Apparently when the Bible was transcribed from Hebrew to Greek, there was a slight error in the translation. Being a woman I would have to say that this is more than slight! The error occurred in Genesis 1:26 and 1:27 "And G-d said, Let us make man in our own image, in the image, after our likeness…" (notice that G-d said "our") " So G-d created Man in his own image, in the image of G-d created he him; male-female created he them". I think it is very clear that this implies that G-d was both male and female!

It seemed to me that the Shekinah has been kept a mysterious secret, as most of the Jewish women that I know had never even heard of Her. The Kaballah teaches that there are both a male and female principal in all creation, and that the entire universe is based upon the principle of sex; and this can be seen in nature everywhere. This is the process of creation, and the Kaballah teaches that the Deities are also dual in nature. Our souls descend to the world in pairs, male and female. They are sometimes referred to as "twin flames". The souls are separated during their descent to earth, but can be reunited and enjoy the same type of marriage that they had above, depending on their state of purity.

Prior to descending onto this earth, each of us made a promise, a "contract" so to speak, which became our "Divine Mission" in life. This was a promise to be an "Expression of God" in physical form, through creativity and service. It is a "Sacred Contract". Once completed, it is our destiny to return to heaven to reunite with God. At times our "Divine Counterpart" chooses not to incarnate – to complete their "mission" from the other side, or it may have already completed its earthly experience, and is now an "Ascended Master". Therefore, our paths may cross in some lifetimes, but not all, depending upon what we choose to learn. Most of us have lived through many incarnations without reuniting with our other half. We have now reached a time in evolution, where we no longer need to find happiness through another person, as we can reunite with our "Divine Counterpart" within ourselves. This can be created by merging our own masculine and feminine energies, and through practicing specific meditations, and working with sacred geometry. When we balance our energies well enough to ascend, we will be able to "hold more light" within our etheric body, and reconnect with our "Twin Flame". We can also ask our "Higher Self" to allow us to reunite with our Twin Flame, if it is in our best and highest good. It is through this divine process of merging our masculine and feminine parts of ourselves, that we reconnect with our Higher Self and our "Soul Family".

So, the Shekinah is the divine counterpart of God, the feminine aspect, also known as the "Divine Bride" and sometimes referred to as the "King's Daughter". She is the "Sister and Mother" of humanity. The Kaballah states that under the words spoken by G-d during the time of creation, it was actually the Shekinah who was the Architect of the Universe. She is known as "The Great Mother in whose fertile womb the Universe was conceived." Most of the visions that Abraham had were actually created by the Shekinah, who lived with Abraham's wife Sarah, in her tent. It is believed that She resides in a house where the couple are sexually active. (This includes you and your soul mate.)

According to the Kaballah, when a child is conceived, the Heavenly King and His Shekinah or "bride" provide the soul while the man and the woman provide the body. The Dieties manifest simultaneously as Mother and Father, creating the spirit. I expect that this is where the Catholic Church came to believe in the trinity. The Christian religion implies that the Holy Spirit is masculine, but the Hebrew word for spirit is "Ruach" which is a feminine noun. So if the Shekinah was living in someone's home, how would you know if she was there?

I was also able to find some information about reincarnation in the Kaballah. I think the following quote explains it quite well: "As long as a person is unsuccessful in his purpose in this world, the Holy One, blessed be He, uproots him and replants him over and over again. (Zohar I 186b) This also confirms that each of us has a purpose, and I was still wondering about mine.

I had always believed in reincarnation anyways, because every year at Passover, when we would celebrate "the Hebrew people being released from slavery in Egypt" we would always pour a glass of wine for Elijah, the great prophet. It is believed that Elijah didn't die, but ascended in the air inside a chariot, and vanished. (This would qualify him as an Ascended Master!) His return has always been associated with the ushering in of the Messianic Age, a time when there would be peace, harmony, and understanding. In the Bible some of the elders ask Jesus "Are you Elijah?" which indicates their belief in reincarnation.

When this all began, one of the questions I had wondered about was why evil exists? I was surprised to find that Kaballah had an answer to that: "If the Lord had not given us the good and evil desires which the scriptures call light and darkness, there would be neither merit or guilt for the created man." Man is a mixture of spirit and matter, and the nature of matter is the will to receive, never to give or bestow. As long as man refuses to share or give, he will be confined to the material world.

The Kaballah also recognizes other belief systems, acknowledging that people of other philosophies can also achieve divine qualities. There are supposedly thirty-six people on the earth, at all times, who are spiritual teachers, and they have daily contact with the

Shekinah. They are referred to as Tzaddikim. According to the "Words of Power" book, the Tzaddakim embody the Tree of Knowledge, (which is part of the Tree of Life) which is necessary to evolve into a more superior state of being. The authors also stated that one of the thirty-six Tzaddakim is considered to be a Priest of Rightousness, similar to a "living Messiah".

The Kaballah teaches that there are Ten Spheres of Sacred Living Fire. These spheres form a pathway of light that connect heaven and earth. The spheres are called "Sephiroth" and they are what form the Tree of Life. Each sphere is named after one of the attributes of God, and is associated with a part of the body. They are known as the ten names, which must never be erased, and each have an Archangel they are associated with. I wondered if the "embodiment of the Tree of Life" was actually a metaphoric statement to imply that the Tzaddakim acquired these "attributes".

"The Tree of Life"

1. Kether / Crown - Archangel Metatron
   Head - the Universe.

2. Chokmah/ Wisdom - Archangel Ratziel
   Left side of face - the Father

3. Binah / Understanding - Archangel Tzaphkiel
   Right side of Face – the Mother

4. Chesed / Mercy – Archangel Tzadkiel
   Left Arm – Forgiveness

5. Geburah/Strength – Archangel Khamiel
   Right Arm - Discipline

6. Tiphereth / Beauty – Archangel Raphael
   Breast - Unity & Perfection

7. Netzach / Victory – Archangel Haniel
   Hips & Legs - Creativity

8. Hod / Glory – Archangel Michael
   Legs &Loins - the Intellect

9. Yesod / Foundation – Archangel Gabriel
   Reproductive organs. Cycles
10. Malkuth / Kingdom – Archangel Sandolphin
    Material World – Shekinah

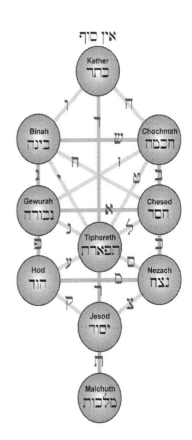

146

Chapter 19

"The Rose and the Cross"

"I could sense someone was trying to wake me. It was in the middle of the night, and when I finally dragged myself out of a very deep sleep, I noticed that I was being shown the inside of a book. At the top of the page on the left was a picture of an Egyptian coffin, and on the other page were the words "Oong Oong". They were explaining to me that I was supposed to get inside the coffin and say those words. Strangely, it wasn't as if I had any choice in the matter, because before I could even think it over, I found myself inside the coffin, with the lid slammed shut! Instantly, the coffin began turning every which way, like the needle on a compass, and then suddenly it seemed to take off, and I found myself flying through space.

In the next scene, I found myself placing the fingers of each hand together, to form an unusual and very complicated configuration and gently raised my arms above my head still holding my fingers together. It was as if I had been trained to do this, and had the strong sense that I knew exactly what I was doing, and as I did this, the coffin gently came to a landing. I found myself on the outside of a building, walking towards the entrance. When I entered the building, I noticed that everything inside was white, and I first noticed a large fountain that was made of elephants forming a circle. They had their tails in the centre and were standing on their rear legs with their front ones up and trunks lifted high in the air. It was a very beautiful fountain. To my left I noticed a room that you had to step up to. I made my way into the room and sat down at a table where my sister and my neice were sitting. In front of me, was a glass box shaped like a rectangle, and in the middle of the box was a pink rose! As soon as I noticed it, I immediately got up and left saying "I have to find the Rosicruscians".

When I got up in the morning, I could remember the experience quite vividly. I had never heard that word before, and wondered if there even was such a word. I had the sensation that these were some type of group. I called the bookstore asking the owner if he knew about anything with that name, and I was amazed once again to discover that he had. He told me that he had several books on the subject. I had to work that day, but couldn't wait to find out who these people were, so I stopped into the bookstore on my way to work. The owner directed me to the back of the store, and after searching through several, selected one called "The Secret Doctrine of the Rosicrucian Order". I picked up the book and was standing at the counter waiting to pay for it, when the man next to me said "It's interesting that you are buying that book." I asked him why, and he said "Look at what you are wearing." I was still working for the cosmetic company, and was wearing a uniform. The dress was navy blue with one large gold button at the neck, which had a circular design of circles within circles. The book happened to be exactly the same colour blue, with the letters of the title written in gold. But just below the title was a gold symbol, which consisted of circles within circles in its design. I laughed and told him that what was even stranger, was the reason I was buying that book, and shared my experience with him. He then said to me "You must read the book "Initiation in the Great Pyramid". It is a story about a woman who recalls a past life in which she was to become a Priestess in the Egyptian Mystery School, and in order to do that, she had to lie inside an Egyptian coffin for three days. The book sounded very interesting, but I was in a hurry, so I bought the little blue book, and went to work.

I soon discovered that the Rosicrucian Order consists of groups of people all over the world, and that it is open to both men and woman. The Order is named after Christian Rosenkreutz and is based on the teachings of the Pharoah Akhnaton who originally held a mystery school inside the Great Pyramid. After doing more research, I learned that there were a lot of very important people who had once belonged to this order, among them Leonardo DaVinci. I also discovered that some people believed that the Pharoah Akhnaton was actually Moses.

I wasn't feeling inclined to join any groups, and eventually I came upon another book called "The True and Invisible Rosicrucian

Order" by Paul Foster Case which spoke about an "invisible" order that when a student is ready, this order can teach one from the "other side". I believe that this was the Order that I was referring to in my "dream". I discovered that their teaching had a lot of information about Kaballah, and one of their symbols was "a rose inside a crystal box". If you take the crystal box that I was shown, and open it up, it would appear as a cross with a Rose in the centre. The symbol for the Rosicrucian Order is a Rose fixed to the centre of a cross. When the box is closed, it represents the "macrocism" and the rose inside the box is the "microcosm". The words macrocosm and microcosm, stem from Greek, and represent a pattern of the universe being reproduced all the way down from the largest scale to the smallest. I have since discovered that the rose represents the Divine Feminine, or the Goddess.

Because a wild rose is made of five petals, and represents the five senses, it sometimes represents our physical body. (Two legs, two arms, and a head) It is one of the symbols used to represent the "word made flesh". All the work of the "Invisible Order" and those who become Rosicrucian's, are directed toward the discovery of "truth", to conform one's life to that Reality, which seemed to be what I was doing. Case goes on to say that the rose is the symbol of the "Secret Church" cherishing the true priesthood "after the Order of Melchizadek" and possessed of the traditional wisdom relating to the G-d of Abraham. This was the first time I came across this "Order" since Val had first mentioned it to me, and I felt that the book was confirming the experiences I was having.

Around this time, I also received a message in which I was told that I should use the Star of David as my banner, so I began using it as part of my email address. As I had basically abandoned my Judaic roots so long ago, it seemed strange for me to be using such a religious symbol, but I was paying attention to what I was being guided to do. I was able to find the true meaning of the symbol in Paul Foster Case's book. He said that the name David means "Love" or "Beloved". The "Star of David" is actually a Hexagram, the interlacing triangles represent the "Law of Love" and the union of all polar opposites throughout the universe. It is a symbol of "cosmic order" as conceived in the Universal Mind prior to the manifestation of man upon earth. It represented the joining together of the masculine and the feminine.

Chapter 20

"The White Rose"

A few days later I went to the book store in search of information on "The Zohar". I found one and had the owner put it aside for me, along with a small crystal. I would return when I got paid.

The following week, just before I awakened, I had another vision:

I was standing between two pillars. As I gazed at the blue sky a perfectly formed long stemmed white rose gracefully appeared in front of me, right between the pillars. A drop of dew fell from it, and then the vision slowly evaporated.

When I woke up, I kept wondering what the vision meant. Later that day, I returned to the book store to get book and the little crystal. The gentleman in the store found the stone, but wasn't able to find the book. As he searched around, a large crystal caught my eye. It was a piece of Selenite, similar in shape to an obelisk, that stood about twelve inches high. It was up on a shelf and it had me totally mesmerized. It seemed to glow as if it had an energy emitting from it. I asked the shopkeeper if I could have a closer look. As he handed this luminescent crystal to me, he said "It's interesting that you're drawn to that crystal. When I asked why, he continued "I'm not sure, but it may be the same crystal that the man who brought it here, Theodore Bromley, was meditating with, when he had the vision which inspired him to write his book called "The White Rose". You can imagine my surprise! I had been shown a "white rose" that very morning, and I knew that I was supposed to purchase the Selenite and the book!

Selenite is a form of "Selenium" the name I had been given in my "Petra" experience, and here I was drawn to that very same crystal, except in a different form. I was still learning about crystals, and it wasn't until years later that I discovered that this white satin luminescent mineral is one of the most powerful crystals available. I read that Selenite "helps us to merge with the energy of the Goddess" and that was exactly what seemed to be happening to me.

I went home with the piece of Selenite and the book called "The White Rose" and a few weeks later, once again, just before waking up, I heard a woman saying *"We could write it together. It all began in Cyprus..."* and the words faded away. As I lay in bed, I couldn't help but wonder whose voice it was that I heard, and what began in Cyprus.

I had visited that island in 1972. I remember it well, because when I arrived, I had the feeling that I had arrived home. I also remember it because I was trying to earn some money along the way, and ended up spending a day modeling sweaters in 120 degree weather! We had visited an ancient Olympian site that day, but I couldn't remember where it had been, or exactly what Cyprus was famous for. I discovered that it was known as the birthplace of Aphrodite. Upon reading about Aphrodite, I almost fell over when I read that her symbol was the "White Rose".

Is it possible that it truly was the Goddess "Aphrodite" that was talking to me? And is it possible that She wanted us to write a book together? Was it the Egyptian Goddess "Isis" that I had seen in my "out of body" experience at the Red Rose City? You can imagine that I found this difficult to comprehend, but then so much was happening to me. I was beginning to believe that perhaps there was more to the ancient biblical stories and mythology than I had believed in the past. I immediately wanted to know as much as possible about Aphrodite, and my thirst for knowledge about the "Divine Feminine" became unquenchable. I didn't know that Aphrodite was also known as Venus, The Goddess of Love. I was able to find a copy of a beautiful painting of Aphrodite by Boticelli, showing her standing on a shell. But, she has also been painted riding a swan or goose. The statue known as "Venus de Milo" by Praxiteles is probably the most recognized rendering of this Goddess. It would seem really miraculous if I really had heard the voice of Aphrodite, and I felt truly blessed and honoured!

The name Aphrodite means "born of foam " and according to Plato there are two goddesses with this name. Aphrodite Urania, the Celestial Goddess of "pure spiritual love" born from the sea, and the younger Aphrodite called Pandemos, a representation of physical love, and the child of Zeus and Diane. There is a temple dedicated to her, which can still be found in Cyprus.

In the book "The White Rose", Theodore Bromley briefly mentioned "The Brotherhood of the White Rose" but I was truly excited when many years later I came across an article written by Dr. Christine Henderson, who wrote about "The Sisterhood of the Rose". She claimed that the Sisterhood is a growing force of women who come from all walks of life that are working individually, or together to assist with the ascension of the planet, and to act as a healing force for mankind, and the earth. They are known as "wisdom-keepers" and are the receptacles for the "Language of Light" which have been entrusted to them throughout time and space. I immediately knew that she was referring to my experiences, and felt an instant connection and bond. Apparently the Sisterhood originated from a sect of the Essene Tribe, with Mother Mary as the Master. There were originally twelve women who formed the basis of the Sisterhood, and each of these women formed twelve more groups, and so on and so forth.

After being shown roses so many times in my dreams and visions, I finally came to the realization that I was possibly a member of this "order", and if so, I felt honoured. Dr. Chris Henderson, states that we have a direct linkage to the universal symbols, which we are guardians of, and that it is our responsibility to release them to those of humanity who are ready and willing to receive them at this time."

Chapter 21

"Platonic Solids"

"Platonic Solids....... Selene!" - Once again, this happened early in the morning just before waking up, and I was trying very hard to understand and remember what it was she was trying to explain. I wasn't sure what Platonic Solids were, and at the same time wondered who "Selene" was.

I already knew that "Selene" meant moon, but upon looking up the name, I discovered that there is also a Goddess by that name. I was overwhelmed! I had experienced seeing the Goddess Isis, and received a message from Aphrodite, and now Selene, who was emphasizing that I learn about Platonic Solids. She had been showing me three globes, one on top of the other. The ones on the top and bottom were smaller than the one in the centre, which had an arm extending from it. She pushed it – to make it rotate in the opposite direction from the smaller orbs. The middle one spinning from right to left. I wasn't sure what she was showing me, but when I tried it, I instantly flew deeply into the cosmos, and was unable to recall what occurred.

I discovered that Platonic Solids are geometric shapes named after Plato, the well-known Greek philosopher, who spent his lifetime searching for "truth". He wrote about many subjects, but his name has become synonymous with "friendship". The word "Platonism" has been described as "transformation via philosophical developments", which he believed could be achieved through the use of specific geometric shapes.

I was surprised to learn that geometric shapes have been part of religious, philosophical, and spiritual cultures throughout history, and that it is often referred to as "Sacred Geometry". I remembered that when I had received the Hebrew Flaming Letters, I had also been shown many geometrical shapes.

The Greeks believed that mathematics held the "key" to religious truth, and therefore found Plato's discovery very interesting. Archaeologists, mathematicians, artists and philosophers have used "sacred geometry" for centuries in their buildings and works of art all over the world. But it was Plato who came to the conclusion that these five shapes were the fundamental building blocks of nature, and assigned to them what he believed to be the essential elements of the universe. Selene was telling me that through the use of Platonic Solids, or Sacred Geometry we can become "one with God". I wondered if the pyramid meditation had something to do with it, since it was geometrical. Platonism can be described as "a desire for union with the beautiful, ascending from human passion to ecstasy".

So here was this word "ascension" once again, and I was wondering if I was excited to receive all the messages and wanted to know more about my new messenger. Perhaps Selene was showing me another method to practice.

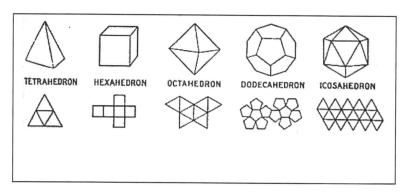

Fire   —   he associated with the Tetrahedron

4 triangular faces, 4 vertices & 4 edges

Earth   —   he associated with the cube Hexahedron

6 square faces, 6 vertices & 6 edges

Air   —   he associated with the Octahedron

8 triangular faces, 6 vertices & 12 edges

Cosmos —   he associated with the Dodecahedron

12 pentagonal faces, 20 vertices & 30 edges

Water   —   he associated with the Icosahedrons

20 triangular faces, 12 vertices & 30 edges

The reason he called the dodecahedron Cosmos is because this shape was so different from all the others, and he felt it must be what the stars and planets were made of. This became the symbol the ancient Greeks used to represent the universe. I noticed that the first four elements (earth, air, fire, & water) were also assigned to the Hebrew name of G-d - Yod Hey Vov Hey.

"The name Selene stems from the Greek word "Selas" which means light, and the Goddess was probably given this name, as the light of the moon is considered to be a reflection of her pale white skin. The Romans called her Luna. According to Greek mythology, Selene can be seen each night traveling across the sky on a silver chariot drawn by two horses. Paintings of her show her as a young woman wearing a long robe carrying a torch, but at times she is seen riding a horse or bull. The Moon Goddess was considered important to the ancient Greeks.

I was surprised to discover that the Egyptians also acknowledged Selene as the Moon Goddess, and that she had an important role in the Egyptian story of creation. According to Egyptian writings, in the very beginning the mighty creator was known as the Sun G-d Ra, and Selene was known as the Moon Goddess. In fact, according to Egyptian mythology, it was because of Selene that we have 365 days of the year, instead of 360.

"Ra was married to the Sky Goddess Nut, but unfortunately Nut was in love with Geb, the Earth. Upon discovering their relationship, Ra

was infuriated, and he became so enraged, that he forbade Nut to give birth to any child on any of the days of the year. At that time, the Egyptian year was made of 360 days. The Sky Goddess, Nut was pregnant at the time, and very upset by this commandment, especially since she wanted and needed to give birth to her child. She begged her friend Thoth to help her. Thoth was the very famous Egyptian Scribe, who looked like a man with the head of a bird called Ibis. He was especially clever, having taught the Egyptians mathematics, and geometry. Thoth knew that Ra's curse must be fulfilled, but he was able to come up with a solution to the problem. At that time, Selene's moon light was so bright that it actually rivaled Ra's light, that of the sun. Thoth made a wager with the Moon Goddess to play a game, and if he won, Selene agreed to give up a portion of her light. As it turned out, Thoth was victorious from the beginning and the game continued until he had won five full days of light. With the extra light, Thoth was able to add five more days to the Egyptian calendar, making the year a total of 365 days. This allowed Nut 5 days when she could give birth to her children, without disobeying Ra. On the first new day, Nut gave birth to Osiris, the lord of the Earth. On the second, Horus was born, Seth came on the third, and on the fourth day, the Goddess Isis was born. Isis' twin sister, Nephthys was born on the fifth and last of these days. Nut became known as the Mother of the Gods, and this is why the moon has less light than the sun, and why each month the moon now wanes".

Chapter 22

"Artemis and Raphael"

In the middle of the night, I heard someone say "Raphael" and I somehow knew (although he didn't announce it) that this was the Archangel. I was then shown a red rose, and a Greek Temple with an American Flag mounted in the centre of the façade. I happened to be in the US at the time, and wondered if that was why I was shown the American Flag. I could see a statue of a woman that I recognized and knew to be "Artemis", which was really strange, because if someone had shown me this same statue during the day, I wouldn't have known who this woman was. But in the dream, I seemed to know perfectly well that it was "Artemis". Then I was shown the Statue of Liberty and I sensed that they were showing me that they were one and the same. That "Liberty" was actually a representation of Artemis. I could also see my little granddaughter, who was eleven months old at the time. She was carrying a red rose. I was taken into the temple that I somehow "knew" was somewhere in the US and a government building. When I went inside I had the feeling that it had been built over a temple dedicated to Artemis. I could feel a different type of energy when I entered the building, and I had the distinct impression that I had entered another dimension. I was shown the caduceus symbol used by the medical profession, which represents healing. Then I experienced the most profound healing sensation throughout my body.

It was February of 2008. I immediately woke up right after this experience. I was in California at the time, visiting with my son and daughter-in-law, and six-month-old granddaughter. Roses once again - they seemed to be showing up fairly often in my dreams. My curiosity had the best of me once again, so I put on my "detective hat" and "googled" the words "Archangel Raphael" and then "Artemis". While I had heard of this Angel, I did not realize that his name actually means "G-d has healed" or "G-d Heals". How amazing! He is the angel that is known as the "Patron Saint" of healers, writers, travelers and the blind. I was astonished to read this, and truly grateful to have had this experience as I was tired of living in pain and hoped that it worked. I had been having problems with arthritis in my knees and my lower back for quite some time, which can be very painful at times.

Raphael is mentioned throughout the Bible several times. He is one of the seven angels who attend the throne of God, and one of the angels who visited the patriarch Abraham, when he was recovering from being circumcised. He presented Noah with a book showing him how to build the ark. Raphael also presented King Solomon with a magic ring. To the Greeks and Romans, Raphael was their "winged messenger god" whom they called Hermes or Mercury, and to the Egyptians he was known as Thoth. So Archangel

Raphael was the same "being" who tricked the Goddess Selene into giving up some of her moon light creating five more days of the year. Raphael's symbol is also the caduceus, the same emblem that represents western medicine, and the one associated with Thoth. The caduceus has two serpents climbing a winged staff, which is what I was shown in my dream.

When I researched the Goddess Artemis, I came across a statue that looked exactly like the one in my dream. She is known as the Virgin Huntress, and is the twin sister to the Greek God, Apollo. It was Artemis who replaced the Goddess Selene as the Moon Goddess. You can imagine how surprised I was to learn this, as I had been editing the chapter about Selene just before I went to bed. I found it interesting that the story I wrote about featured Thoth & Selene - who appeared to me as Raphael and Artemis.

Artemis is sometimes depicted in quite a different way from most of the Greek Goddesses, her legs bound with rope to make her appear pillar-like, and her arm resting on the "winged staff of healing". Artemis was associated with Cybele as well as Diana. There was even a "cult" named after her.

The Temple of Artemis, also known as the Temple of Diana, took 120 years to build. It was completed around 550 BC at the City of Ephesus under the Persian Empire, which is now present-day Turkey. Nothing remains of the original temple, but it was once considered to be the most beautiful of the Seven Wonders of the

Ancient World. The temple was filled with artwork and statues depicting many different beliefs, which made it a place of worship for everyone. The people who built the City of Ephesus, were the Amazons, and it is believed that they would also visit the temple. An inscription found on the Greek Island of Crete refers to her as "the Cretan Lady of Ephesus, the Light-Bearer" which made me think that perhaps she is also the one that "Liberty" represents.

Unfortunately, the temple was destroyed on July 21, 356 BC by Herostratus, the evening that Alexander the Great was born. Artemis, is known to watch over babies, and especially at the time of birth, and supposedly she was too preoccupied with Alexander's delivery to save her burning temple. Alexander later offered to pay for the Temple's rebuilding, but the Ephesians refused. The temple was eventually rebuilt, but destroyed once again. I had seen my little granddaughter in the vision, and I wondered if I was being shown that she too was under the watchful eye of Artemis.

My mind went back to the building I had seen. The name "Library of Congress" suddenly came to me. It just "popped" into my head. I have never been to Washington, so I had never seen this building, and knew nothing about it, other than it being some type of government building. So I searched for some information, and found a photo. I was amazed to see a building that looked very much like a Greek Temple, and there in the centre was an American Flag, as I had been shown in the vision.

I learned that Thomas Jefferson, a Rosicrucian, was very influential with the building of The Library of Congress, and many of the books in there, were once owned by him. I had never seen photographs of this place before, so I was truly impressed when I found several photos showing the insides of the building, which is a magnificent "work of art". It is filled with giant archways, and domed ceilings adorned with paintings and carvings of angels. The building has many pillars and statues. It is truly one of the most beautiful structures I have ever seen, and according to the description of the Temple of Artemis, I would have to say, that this surely would be its match. Inside the building there is a statue of a "Light-Bearer" (as Artemis was "referred to" in Crete) and on top of the Capitol Dome is a statue called "Lady Freedom" - which I would think represents Liberty. I learned that the Statue of Liberty's official name is "Liberty Enlightening the World".

Was I being shown that the Library of Congress, or the US government's foundation was built on the latter? Liberty enlightening the world? Was there some type of connection to the Divine Feminine? Was it built upon some type of Temple? I don't know, and perhaps I never will, but for me, it seemed that way, and it was "a place of healing".

Chapter 23

"Rosalee, Rosalye and Rosaline"

"Rosalee, Rosalye and Rosaline" These were the names that I heard in the middle of the night. I had been keeping track of the many dreams and visions I was experiencing, and I thought that I was being given a name for the document that was quickly growing into a manuscript, so I chose Rosaline, with the name Temple to go along with it. At the same time, I was also shown a golden triangle with an intricate design delicately engraved inside, and I could hear someone say "finish Solomon's circle to the right". I had no understanding of what this could possibly mean, but I could see some very old knights digging in the earth. I strongly sensed that they were somewhere in the holy land, where the original temple had been built, and not in England where I associated knights to be. These knights were wearing suits of armor that were completely made of chains or "mail" - very plain, and not decorative at all, which led me to believe that they must have been some of the very first knights, that wore this type of armor. I had this "knowingness" of exactly where these scenes were taking place, which I somehow knew that they were near the ancient temple site in Jerusalem. They were digging in the earth, as if they were looking for something.

I couldn't help but wonder if it was an ancient memory from a past life. It wasn't until after Val had loaned me a book called "The Hiram Kay" by Robert Lomas and Chrostopher Knight, that I learned that about the place called "Roslin Chapel" which is located in Edinborough Scotland. It was built on a piece of land, with the name "Roslin" which is known to be a leyline. This book confirmed what I had been shown in my dream/vision. They said that while in Jerusalem, some knights had been digging in the area where Solomon's Temple had originally stood, and they discovered several objects. Among them were the blueprints for King Solomon's Temple, which they brought back to Scotland. Rosaline Chapel was built according to these blueprints, which makes it a complete replica of the original temple. As well, some people believe that this is where other sacred objects may be hidden, including "the Lost Arc".

I learned that the knights that are associated with this particular chapel are called "The Knight's Templar". After learning all of this, and choosing the name "Rosaline Temple" it became obvious to me, and to others, that I must have been experiencing some past life memories, and that somehow I was connected to all of this. I recalled the "message" I had received on the radio so many years ago, and couldn't help but wonder, if this was why he had mentioned Edinborough, Scotland.

In the morning, after hearing the names, I called my friend Rosalee, asking her what her thoughts were about using another name for the book. She told me that she didn't think there was anything wrong with it, as lots of authors used a "nom de plume". As hers was one of the names mentioned, she informed me that all of those names mean "Flower of Life", which sounded very nice to me, but at that time, I had no understanding of the phrase.

I had a meeting in Vancouver, and on my way home, I stopped into the bookstore to see if they had any information about "Solomon's circles". I was totally shocked when the man brought out a book that was filled with nothing except Solomon's circles! But it was all about magic, and I didn't feel qualified to perform any type of magic, and to be truthful about the matter, the whole idea frightened me. But while I was in the bookstore, I noticed another book with a golden triangle on the cover, which instantly jogged my memory of the one I had seen in my dream. I mentioned this to the man, explaining that in the vision, it had an intricate design inside. Immediately, he said to me "oh, that sounds like one of the symbols associated with the "Flower of Life". I was quite surprised to hear that expression once again, within such a short period of time, and then he showed me a drawing that his son had been working on just that morning. I felt that I was being given confirmation that the name was quite suitable.

Then, he brought me a book to look at, and it was the first time I had come across this book, which confirmed a lot of the experiences that I was having. It was called "The Ancient Secret of the Flower of Life". It was as if I was solving some type of mystery, and the synchronicities were quite overwhelming. When I opened the book, the first thing I saw was the drawing of a man on the wheel, similar to the one I had seen of my son standing on the wheel in my "Petra" experience. Inside the book were photographs and drawings of Angels, along with Egyptian symbols, and spaceships. I had been seeing a lot of spaceships in my dreams, and if I didn't mention it before, I had even found myself flying inside them. So seeing all of these images in one book, confirmed for me that someone else was having similar experiences to mine.

The book was written by Drunvalo Melchizadek, who had been teaching a meditation that would activate something that was called your Merkabah or "light body" and by practicing it, you could have an experience with God. I never did learn this particular meditation, because I had been having extraordinary results from my own meditation. It was my personalized version of the meditation from Archangel Michael, in "The Crystal Stair" which I have included at the end of this book.

It took me awhile to discover that I was being taught a very ancient and sacred teaching. I kept asking my "guides" what my purpose was. The reply I received was "The Universal Flower Language". Upon asking a friend what she thought that meant, she replied "it must be part of "The Flower of Life" teachings."

It was after reading Drunvalo's book, that I learned that the name Rosaline, in Scottish Gaelic, actually means "ancient knowledge handed down the generations". As well, the expression "rose line" is used to describe the "meridians of the body" and "leylines of the earth" and this was exactly what this teaching was about. It was about reconnecting our bodies with the energy of the earth by traveling to key places, and through the combination of specific types of meditation along with the use of sacred geometry, those areas would be activated.

Chapter 24

"An Amazing Maze"

Val told me that everything in the universe is made of energy, including everything we think, everything we say, and everything we do. She also told me that everything works in a circle, so that if we think positive thoughts, say positive things, and do positive deeds, that all that will eventually return to us. She also explained that everywhere we go, our etheric bodies (energy body) gather information, especially when we visit sacred spots, where many people have visited to pray, or perform spiritual ceremonies. I gathered that when I had visited Cyprus and had gone to some of the ruins there, my etheric body had collected some of this information, and perhaps this was why I was able to connect with Aphrodite. Val explained that even when we meet or talk with ordinary people, our energy bodies exchange certain information, which may have an impact on us. I recalled that I had read that in "Embraced by the Light" by Betty Jane Eadie. Although I understood the concept, it was shortly after she had reminded me of it, that I had such an experience.

I happened to be browsing through an antique shop, when I came upon a set of salad spoon and forks, that looked quite old. What I found fascinating were the Egyptian symbols on them. I was staring at them, when suddenly the shop owner came up beside me asking what it was that I found so intriguing. I explained to him that I had been having many visions of Egypt and it was the symbols that had drawn me to them. He noticed that when I turned to look at him, I was staring at the necklace he was wearing, which had a small leather bag hanging from it. "I'm a medicine man." He explained and then he went on to say that he also had visions, and that they had begun when he was thirteen years old. He asked me if I knew what had triggered them, and I said that I had no idea. He then invited me over to browse through some Egyptian papyrus paintings that he had in the store.

As we browsed through the papyrus, he noticed that I was wearing an amethyst ring, and asked me how I got it, and where it was from. I told him that I had bought it when I was in Mexico, about six months before, and that I had been very drawn to it. He showed me that he too was wearing an amethyst ring, and that he had been given it for his thirteenth birthday. He seemed to think that rings had something to do with the visions. I am now aware that this particular crystal is connected to the area known as our "crown chakra" located at the top of our heads. It is where the "soft spot" is on babies' heads, and is the area that connects with God. (It sounds like He or She has a sense of humour, since it appears that we were specifically created with a "soft spot" for God".)

As I thumbed through the Papyrus I noticed that several of the Egyptian paintings showed deities with snakes protruding from their foreheads. I now understand that the Egyptians headdresses with the upraised snakes on top of the foreheads, represent someone who has mastered the kundalini energy that sits at the base of the spine. The priests and priestesses of ancient times used to practice bringing it up the spine, through the chakras, or energy gateways of the body, to have an experience with God. This was also practiced for healing, and this is where the "caduceus" originated from. It represents the two little snakes called the Ida and Pengala that entertwine through the chakras (gateways) of the body, up the winged staff.

I asked the "medicine man" what he thought the snake represented, and he explained to me that they signify "knowledge" and then he reminded me about the story of Moses and the burning bush.

In the story of Moses, the Hebrew people were slaves in the land of Egypt. During that time, Pharoah announced that all male Hebrew babies were to be killed. To save his life, Moses was hidden amongst the bulrushes, where he was found by one of Pharoah's wives, who decided to keep him as one of her own. Moses's sister Miriam befriended the woman, asking if she should find a "wet nurse" for the baby, and Pharoah's wife agreed. Of course, Miriam brought her mother , and this was how learned that he was really a "Hebrew". As an adult, he became alarmed at how badly Pharaoh was treating the Hebrew people. Eventually, Moses became so enraged at one of the guards who was "whipping" a Hebrew slave, that he lashed out at the Egyptian, killing him in his anger. After realizing what he had done, he fled into the desert where he stayed for 40 years. This was where met the man named Jethro, married one of his daughters, and had children. One day while tending some sheep, Moses came to the "Mountain of God" – Mount Horeb. There was a "burning bush" and Moses heard a voice calling to him. He was told to take off his sandals, as he was standing on holy ground. (It is believed by some that it was the Shekinah that was speaking to Moses.) He was instructed to return to Egypt and tell Pharoah to set the Hebrew people free. Moses was to lead the Hebrew people out of Egypt to Israel, the promised land. Moses was a very humble person, and also didn't speak very well. He protested to G-d stating that Pharoah would never believe that he was sent by G-d to do this. The voice assured Moses that God's presence would be with him. He was then instructed to bring his brother Aaron to speak for him. Then G-d told Moses to throw his shepherd's staff to the ground, which he did, and G-d turned it into a snake, and then back into a staff once again. G-d assured Moses that he would accompany him.

Moses humbly accepted his role as God's chosen one, and asked his brother to join him as he set out on his journey back to Egypt. When he finally met with Pharoah, he proclaimed that the G-d of Israel wanted Pharoah to release his people. Of course Pharoah protested, saying that he did not know this God, and he wouldn't let the people of Israel go! This was when Moses threw his staff onto the ground, and it instantly turned into a snake. The Egyptian priests were able to perform the same feat with their staffs, but the snake belonging to Moses quickly devoured theirs, showing that this G-d of the Hebrew people was more powerful than those of the Egyptians. Pharoah still wasn't convinced, and It wasn't until after ten different plagues came upon the Egyptian people, that he finally agreed to let the Hebrew people go."

That night, I had another vision, and I truly believe that my meeting with the medicine man triggered the vision.

I had been asleep and felt that I had been awakened in the middle of the night, to hear a voice say "In order to have "Kingdomship" you must have knowledge." Suddenly I found myself standing in front of a very large wall, which was completely covered in a mosaic design. It looked like hundreds of tiny little tiles. Instantly, the heads of three little snakes appeared to come out of the wall, with their cobra heads upraised like the ones on Egyptian headdresses, suddenly they retracted back into the wall. The profile of a giant wheel instantly appeared within the wall, slowly rotating, and as it turned I had the sensation that I had somehow activated it. It stopped at just the right place, and an opening appeared. I began walking though what appeared to be a long hallway, and I couldn't help but notice that the walls were covered in hieroglyphics and ever so often I would turn one way, and then another. It was some kind of a maze, and I seemed to know exactly how to make my way through it. When I finally got to the centre, I found myself inside a large room, which was also covered in thousands of hieroglyphics, and this room was shaped like a Star of David. I remember saying to someone, I am thirsty, and they told me to get a drink of water, which I did. When I returned, I closed my eyes and once again I saw myself standing in front of the mosaic wall. But this time, the face of Mother Mary came out from the wall and another entrance opened. I was able to make my way through this hallway, as well, and eventually entered another room, which was shaped like a five pointed star. When I looked up, I could see a dome that was opening like the petals of a flower, and I could see the sky which was filled with a circle of very large Angels. They were all looking at me, and then I had the sensation of traveling through space with these Angels, but could not remember anymore of the dream.

All in all, it was quite an a "mazing" experience and I felt that somehow the medicine man and I had an "energy exchange" that triggered the dream. Of course, I wondered about the message. *"in order to have Kingdomship, you must have knowledge"*. I had been reading the "Keys of Enoch" which is also called "The Book of Knowledge" written by J. J. Hurtak. I found it a very difficult book to understand, but a friend of mine had loaned it to me, as she felt that my experiences were similar to what was described in the book. At the back of the book was a Glossary, so I decided to look up "Knowledge". I was surprised to read the following: *"An emanation from the Diety that enables one to create a pathway or flow of consciousness to travel through the myriad heavens. The vehicle of Wisdom – (Sophia) The Bride of God, the feminine side of the*

Godhead". Interestingly, it seemed that the word *Sophia* was from Kaballah. I seemed to be having not only Jewish experiences, but Christian, Egyptian, and Greek mythological ones, as well.

I was also curious about Amethyst, and learned that the word stems from the Greek word "amethystus". During ancient times, the Greeks and Romans would crush this stone, in order to use it to protect themselves from intoxication. There were even cups made of this crystal, as the stone can help overcome addictions. This is how it came to known as the "Sobriety Stone". (I particularly found that interesting because I was drawn to it while vacationing in Mexico the very day that I decided to give up smoking.)

The stone's colours range from the palest of mauve to the deepest violet, and some forms can be found in beautiful shades of pale green. They say that the deeper the colour, the stronger the affect. It was actually the deep violet colour that attracted me to it, when I first saw it. The stone is actually a form of quartz, and according to Greek mythology, it's "royal hue" came about in a very unique way.

The Greek G-d known as Dionysis, the G-d of Wine *(and sometimes mischief)* became annoyed with the Moon Goddess Artemis, sometimes referred to as the "virgin huntress". In order to punish her, he decided to attack one of the virgin maidens attending her shrine. Dionysis set his sacred tigers upon this virgin, but in order to protect her, Artemis instantly petrified the virgin, turning her into a statue of sparkling clear quartz. Mourning over the maidens demise,

Dionysis poured his cup of wine over the statue, infusing it with it's deep purple hue. The name of this virgin maiden was "Amethyst" and that is how the stone got its' name.

They say that it is the stone to wear, when dealing with stressful situations, and it can also help to create abundance in ones' life. It's serene energy gives one the feeling of contentment, and can help during times of great sadness. As I personally discovered, Amethyst will enhance our psychic abilities. It can help to open our "crown" chakra, allowing us to connect with the Angelic Realm, and the Divine. It is supposed to be a good stone to use during meditation or to place under your pillow to enhance your "dream time". I also learned that it can be worn for protection. I was surprised to learn that it is the stone often worn by mystics and spiritual healers, as it assists in the ability to heal. I was quite impressed with the list of ailments it could help with, as well. It is recommended to help pain relief, as well as migraine headaches, fibromyalgia, arthritis, chronic fatigue and sleeplessness, diabetes, and circulatory problems. It has also been recommended for endocrine system problems, immune system deficiency, asthma, phobias, PMS, menopause, and to prevent miscarriages. As I discovered, it is used to open the "crown chakra" as well as the "third eye" and the heart. I later learned that it works especially well with Selenite, the other stone I was led to, as the two together seem to "activate" one another.

Chapter 25

"Lamad - Knowing"

My husband kissed me on the back of the neck, and told me he liked my perfume. He asked me what it was called. I said "Knowing". He repeated "What is it called?" I answered again, repeated the word, and then heard him say "Hmm - spring has finally sprung!" I noticed a Hebrew letter suspended in the air, beautifully formed, and perfectly created from a flame, and then someone said "Lamad".

I woke up with this Hebrew Flaming Letter on my mind, along with the word. I had learned the Hebrew Aleph/Bet as a child, but had only been taught the name of the letters, and shown what each of them looked like. But since I began having the visions, I discovered that each letter has a very special meaning, and assigned a specific number.

Upon looking up the letter Lamad, I was shown that the word meant exactly what my husband (in my dream) was telling me, that it represents knowledge or "knowing". I was amazed to learn that this particular letter meant so much.

Lamad is situated in the very centre of the Hebrew alphabet, and is the tallest. It rises above all of the others, representing man's desire to "reach towards the heavens" to understand the universe. (I felt like this letter represented me!) If you take the letters directly in front, and after Lamad, the word King can be read. Because of the letter being in the very middle of the alphabet, the "heart" of the Aleph Bet, it represents "heart knowledge".

Love

Good Conscience

Sincere Faith

The Hebrew word for "heart" actually says "two lamads". If you take one of two lamads, and turn it around, it will create a mirror image, appearing to look like an open heart – the sages say it is "open to receive God's love".

The great teachers, throughout centuries, have taught that the tiny letter at the very top of the Lamad that forms part of the letter, is the smallest of all the Hebrew letters, and represents the humbleness of God, making himself or herself small enough to fit into our hearts. If you look at the Hebrew Bible called the Torah, in the very centre of the scroll, you will find the words "the heart that understands wisdom" – this is the true meaning of "Lamad".

The letter means both to learn and to teach. It represents a great teacher that reaches down to teach us the mysteries of God, and to make us instrumental in creating a new heaven and a new earth.

I read that the number associated with this letter is 30, the same amount of the days of the month, and of a lunar cycle, which coincides with women's natural cycles as well. Therefore, the letter also stands for a feminine being and taking part in "creation".

I found the information interesting, especially since I had previously heard the words "in order to have Kingdomship, you must have knowledge" and was shown the face of Mother Mary. Is this who was reaching down to teach me? Could this truly be possible?

When I shared some of these experiences with some friends, I was often asked if I was scared, but the outpouring of love that I received was so profusely strong, that I had absolutely no fear. I felt completely bathed in the feeling of love, and when the Angels poured "perfume" into my third eye explaining that this was "The Zohar" the most wonderful feeling came over me.

I finally found a book on "The Zohar" or "Book of Splendour" as it is called in English, and I learned that it is, considered by some, to be the most sacred book of all. The book talked about something called "the Merkabah" which means "chariot" in Hebrew, as well as the Divine Feminine, whom they called the "Shekinah" and she was often referred to as "Divine Splendour" or Divine Radiance". Interestingly, the information was hidden for over eight hundred years inside a cave near a town in the Middle East called Meron. The pages were discovered by a young Arab, who took them to the market, where he sold them for wrapping paper! Luckily, a few sheets fell into the hands of a man who was able to read them, and he discovered that the information was of great significance. The book has been the subject of controversy among philosophers for centuries. Prior to this, the teachings had been passed down "verbally" or were received "directly from God". When the information was finally written, the stories were dictated by one Rabbi to another, Rabbi Shimon told them to Rabbi Abba and the information was written in such a way, that only those who had reached a certain level of spirituality would be able to comprehend the information.

The Zohar was to remain hidden until the time known as the "return of the Messiah" had arrived. The Shekinah is considered to be the "bride of God" or the feminine aspect known as "the G-d who dwells within". It is a feminine word, and stems from the Hebrew word Shakhan, which means "to dwell" or "to live with" and sometimes it is used in the context as "to pitch one's tent." In the story of Abraham, it states that the Shekinah lived with his wife Sarah "inside her tent". When Moses received the ten commandments, he was also given instructions to build an Ark that was to house the Menorah (candelabra) and the Divine Shekinah.

I had previously read about the Ark being built, and the Menorah being placed inside, but I had never heard of the Shekinah, and even though I am Jewish I had never known that there was a "feminine aspect of G-d ". I remember from the biblical story that they carried this Ark wherever they went, until King David finally placed it inside the temple that was built by King Solomon in Jerusalem, where it was placed inside the "Holy of Holies." The temple was eventually destroyed, and it was during the destruction of the second temple that the Ark was stolen. But I have read that when the Hebrew people fled, the Shekinah went with them.

I believe today that the Goddess expresses herself in many ways, and although I am not an authority, it could be that Isis, Aphrodite, Mary, Artemis, and the Shekinah are possibly one and the same. There are similar goddesses in other civilizations. Herodotus implies that the story of Aphrodite stems from the ancient Semitic "goddess of love" called Ishtar-Astarte. I feel privileged that I have been blessed with their presence.

Chapter 26

"Creating Change"

Val also taught me about prayer. We had been talking about energy and "creating change". She said that we can change *some* of the things in our life, but not all, because Earth is basically a school, and we come here to learn. We are also given "free will", but it is important to remember that we are not supposed to interfere with someone else's lessons.

She explained that before we are born, G-d or Goddess takes us all around the world, showing and teaching us everything, allowing us to choose what it is that we would like to experience in this lifetime. For example, some of us may want to know about love or compassion, or perhaps we will want to experience wealth or fame. So if, for instance, the lesson is about compassion, it's possible that someone around us may become sick, or we may be the "teacher" of that lesson, and become ill ourselves. In that case, we would learn about "pain and suffering". Some of us may have our hearts broken, and some may not realize what happiness is, until we suffer some sort of loss or hardship.

We also choose the families that we are born into, and apparently everything is "pre-arranged and agreed to" prior to our coming to earth. When we are born, we are at first influenced by our parents and the people around us, who come into our lives, as well as our environment. Our upbringing can be completely different depending on where we choose to live, for example Canada, as opposed to Peru or the Middle East. Our lives would be influenced by the different climates and belief systems, etc. Once we reach a certain age, we begin to make certain choices for ourselves. Every once in awhile, we reach a "fork in the road" and have to decide which route to take, which may or may not change our lives drastically. Whether we continue with our education, or decide to get involved with drugs or alcohol, or who we choose to be friends with. All these things affect our lives. But Val said that throughout our lives, we always have a choice, and we have the ability to change things, if it is "for our best and highest good".

Val said that prayer is basically "talking to God" and that we each have a "spark of the Divine" within us, which means that we are co-creators with God. She explained that we shouldn't be asking for something when we pray, but "thanking God" for all the things that we already have, and for the things that we don't. For instance, if you really wanted to go to Hawaii or some other exotic place for a holiday, you might say "if it is for my best and highest good, thank you G-d for this wonderful Hawaiian vacation" and then you might want to visualize yourself there. In this way, you are behaving as if you already own it, and you are co-creating with God.

I also learned that if we are not happy with something that is happening in our life, then we can change it, by "refusing to accept it" and thinking about what it is we would like to see or have happen. I began to use some of these "techniques".

I had one incident with my husband, which worked amazingly well. He had asked me to put all of our "gas charges" on one specific credit card, to keep track of how much gas we were using. I agreed that it was a good idea and began doing this. A few weeks later, as I was getting ready to go to work, my husband was busy going through our bills. "I thought I asked you to put all the gas on one credit card" he said, in a "not so nice" tone. I told him that I had been doing just that. "Then why do I see gas charges on our Visa when I asked you *specifically* to use the Mastercard for gas?" I said that as far as I knew, I HAD been using the Visa, but maybe I left the card home one day, and had to use the other one. He said that there wasn't just one charge, but several. Anyways, we got into a big argument about it, and I really hated his whole attitude.

Then I remembered what Val had said. I was in the washroom, putting on my make-up, so I looked into the mirror and said very firmly: "I REFUSE TO ACCEPT THIS AS MY REALITY" and thought that he should apologize to me. A few minutes later, he came to the door and said "I'm sorry, you did use the right card. I just noticed the note at the bottom of the bill." He showed me the bill, and in very small print at the bottom of the bill it said: "we apologize for using Visa stationery, but we ran out of Mastercard paper". It appeared that both credit card companies were using the same billing company. Honestly, in the few minutes between his comments, and my refusal to accept his behaviour, the message seemed to have magically appeared on the bill.

Val also explained that some of us have agreed to come here to teach about a "higher consciousness" a "higher learning" which is about "the Divine". This is known as our "Sacred Contract". She said that when we begin to fulfill this contract, that all the pieces of the puzzle begin to fall into place, and everything will "flow". We are generally shown this through coincidences and synchronicity.

I was shown this on the "physical" level a few days later. I was having lunch with Rachel, a friend of mine, who had also been my partner, when we were selling real estate. We met at one of the hotels in the area, and the two of us spent an enjoyable afternoon, visiting with each other, and catching up on each other's lives.

After telling Rachel about some of the dreams and visions I had been experiencing, she told me about a set of books called the "Life and Teaching of the Masters of the Far East". She said that she had just finished reading the whole series, and thought I would find them quite interesting. The "series" is written by a man by the name of Baird T. Spalding, who was one of eleven people that journeyed to the "far east" in 1894. Rachel said that the group traveled through the Himalayas for three and a half years, meeting with whom they referred to as "Great Masters". They originally set out to learn about their teachings, but experienced many miraculous events along the way. As soon as she began telling me about the books, I wanted to read them. Rachel said that she would loan me her set, but for some reason, I felt that I wanted to have my own. Rachel immediately told me that they were really hard to come by. I wrote down the name of the series, and told her that if it was meant for me to have a set of my own that I would find one, but if not, I would borrow hers.

When we left the hotel, I went over to "Phoenix", the metaphysical bookstore where I seemed to be spending a lot of money those days. I walked in, note in hand, and began looking through the bookshelves. Having no success, I approached the woman behind the counter, inquiring as to whether she had ever heard of this collection. She read the note and then looked up at me asking if I had ordered them. I told her that I had only just heard about them over lunch. The woman's eyes widened as I spoke. She said "they arrived twenty minutes ago..." She went on to explain that she had actually ordered them a long time ago, and had been expecting them to arrive months ago, but they had only just arrived." We were both amazed and the synchronicity! Of course, I knew that the books were meant for me. The stories contained in this collection were quite amazing and some of the most fascinating I have come across. Mr. Spalding explains that there are many Masters who are assisting and guiding the destinies of mankind. He also states that while the Masters accept Buddha as the "Way to Enlightenment" it is their belief that "Christ" is a "state of consciousness or enlightenment".

Chapter 27

"Crystal Heads"

I was taken "out of body" traveling to many deserts all over the world, collecting many "keys and codes" in my "etheric" body. At the time, I didn't know what an "etheric" body was, yet I seemed to have some type of awareness of it, and it is my understanding that it is a replica of our physical body, except that it is made up of energy. Anyways, I had the sensation that by traveling to these places, my energetic body was collecting some sort of information. It was during one of these journeys that I had an experience in which I was shown two crystal heads. Many people are familiar with crystal skulls, but at the time I had this experience, I had never heard of them. In the vision, I was shown two "heads" that appeared to be made of crystal. I could have thought they were made of glass, but I seemed to just "know" that these were made of pure crystal. I had the impression at the two heads somehow belonged together, as if they were twins. Each "head" looked like a perfect sculpture of a male between the ages of thirty and forty, with short, fairly modern hairstyles, but strangely, there were no bodies attached to them. I was shown both heads at the same time, first from one angle, and then another. When this was done, a ray of light suddenly emanated from the foreheads of each of these heads, directly into my third eye. It was as if I somehow activated them, and then a stream of information was downloaded into my "etheric" body. I had the feeling that this was happening for a specific purpose, and that I, myself, had been the one that originally put the information into the heads in the first place, perhaps in a past life, but I wasn't sure. I didn't seem to have access to the information, but I believed that whatever came into my being, was placed there for a specific purpose.

I later met someone who had asked me if I had ever had any visions about Crystal Skulls. I shared with her my experience, and she shared with me that she had actually seen a very famous skull called "The Mitchell-Hedges" crystal skull, and had been given the opportunity to spend several days with the owner, meditating with it. This was the first time I had ever heard of crystal skulls, but later learned that the Mayans refer to them as "Crystal Heads" which I found interesting, because that was what I had been shown, not skulls.

Of course quartz crystal is used today in watches, and can be found in our computers, as well as other communication devices. On the website called crystalskulls.com, the author states that ancient man may not have had the technology that we have today, but they were aware of the "information-storing" properties of quartz crystal. It is believed that the crystal skulls that are now re-surfacing, carry important information. He states that if one small chip can hold thousands of photographs, songs, movies, etc., just imagine how much information could be stored in a piece of quartz the size of a human head. This confirmed my experience that the "heads" contained information. This confirmed my thoughts about the heads I had seen, that some type of information had been "downloaded" into my third eye.

Some people believe that there is some type of connection between the crystal skulls and the Galactic Alignment of the Mayan Calendar in December 2012. There is a legend that states "at a pivotal time in humanity's history, the 13 crystal skulls will be reunited to awaken a new era - transforming from an old paradigm into a new world". Some people are under the impression that there may be more than 13 of these ancient crystal skulls -- that there may be four sets of 13 heads.

The spiritual advisor, Patricio Dominguez writes: "The crystal skulls are complete depositories of knowledge and each skull contains a particular area of specialized information - like a living library. He believes that each SKULL IS LIKE ONE VOLUME IN A SET OF ENCYCLOPEDISA, And that we will only be able to extract all the knowledge from the skulls once they are all assembled together.

Chapter 28

"The Pyramid of Giza"

My "out of body" travels continued, and eventually I was taken to the Great Pyramid of Giza. Once inside, a huge "beam of light" suddenly came out of the ground, sprout wings and began twirling, just like a rotor in a car, except this was giant sized. It was as if my presence had activated something inside the pyramid, and I sensed that the information I had collected in my "etheric" body while traveling to the deserts, and the information "downloaded" from the crystal heads had something to do with this "activation".

When I returned the following night, the pyramid and Sphinx were covered in gold. In the vision, the Sphinx had two huge beautiful golden wings, that reached up high towards the sky. I seemed to instinctively know what to do, and quickly took the wings off the Sphinx and placed them vertically onto one of the sides of the Pyramid. Instantly twelve sets of doors opened simultaneously, and then I found myself inside the pyramid, in the area known as the King's Chamber. The following night I returned once again, but this time, I found myself inside a large room beneath the Sphinx and the pyramid. I wasn't sure how I knew where I was, but seemed to "intuitively" know this, and sensed that the rooms were somehow *connected to each other. This time I noticed a large golden fish, and a large golden bird, which my presence, once again, seemed to activate and they suddenly came alive. I found myself gravitating towards a large statue, which felt somewhat like a magnet pulling me towards it, and unexpectedly found myself inside this statue, saying the word "Arcturius". I had never heard of this word before, but in the dream, I was very sure of what I was saying. Within seconds I discovered that I was flying inside a tiny spaceship traveling through space. Eventually I entered a much larger vehicle, which I believed to be the mother ship. I recall looking out the window and seeing what looked like millions of stars, and strangely, I said to myself "This must be the Milky Way", which I seemed to recognize, as if I was a "frequent flyer" through that particular area, and had been there before. I flew through space towards Arcturius, a place I had no knowledge of, at least in my "three dimensional" life.*

Later I learned that this is the fourth brightest star in the sky, and the brightest one in the constellation known as Bootes, the Hunter. The name comes from the Greek word "Arktouros" which means "Guardian of the Bear ". It was named that because it is situated next to the constellations of the Big and Little Bears, Ursa Major and Ursa Minor. I have since felt that there is a connection to this star and King Arthur, whose nickname was "the Bear". Edgar Cayce spoke about this Star, and believed that it was one of the most advanced civilizations in this galaxy. He states that it exists in the "fifth dimension" and is considered to be the "prototype" for Earth's future. It is also an energy gateway through which humans pass during death and re-birth. Arcturius is the place where individuals pass, when they choose whether or not to return to the "Earth-Sun system" or other star systems. It is believed by many, that it is the Arcturians that are creating the crop circles all over the earth.

On further investigation, I learned that this particular star is looked upon with great respect. This star can be seen in temples along the Nile, and is considered to be an "objects of worship". The Egyptians called it Smat, which means "one who rules, subdues, and governs" or "the coming one" – Bau. The Arabic refer to it as "the keeper of the heaven"- Haris-el-sema. It seems that this Star is very special. At the time I had this experience, I knew nothing about Arcturius, and have no idea how the name came to me, but I expect that the knowledge came either from a past life, or my "unseen" guides.

Of course, it also seemed strange that there would be a "spaceship" hiding beneath the pyramid, and I chalked it up to being a "dream" and everyone knows how some dreams don't make much sense. But eventually I came across some information in a book that said there actually is supposed to be a spaceship hidden beneath the Giza pyramid. You can't imagine how shocked I was when I discovered the following information. Drunvalo Melchizadek wrote in his book "The Ancient Secret of the Flower of Life" about a channeled message from his guide Thoth, the Ancient Egyptian God, "that approximately one mile beneath the Sphinx there is a round room with a flat floor and a flat ceiling. Inside this room is the oldest synthetic object on Earth. According to Thoth, though even he can't prove it, this object goes back 500 million years when "that which led to human life" began. The object is about two city blocks in size, it's round like a disk and has a flat bottom and top. It's unusual in that its skin is only three to five atoms thick. Its top and bottom surfaces have a certain pattern on it, which is five atoms thick; everywhere else it's only three atoms thick. And it's transparent - you can see right through it - almost like it's not there. This is a ship, but it has no motors of visible form of power. He goes on to say that it is actually propelled by thoughts and feelings, and is designed to connect with and extend our own living Merkabah, our light body. The ship is connected directly to the spirit of the Earth, and it is also mentioned in Dr. Michael Doreal's book called the "The Emerald Tablets".

The following night, the vision continued. My guides kept telling me to "change my pyjamas" to put myself into a state of pure love. I seemed to understand that by doing this, it would allow me to raise my vibration to a level high enough to travel further. They kept showing me kittens, which I love so dearly, and it helped me be to become an "expression of love". Eventually I was able to make myself "light" enough to experience this higher dimension, and I was taken to another gateway, the thirteenth one, which had a huge Golden Arch. It reminded me of the Archway between Canada and the United States, but it appeared even greater in size. I was greeted at the door by some very important people, to say the least,

St. Francis D'Assisi, Mother Mary, Joan of Arc, and Laura Secord, who I refer to as the "Chocolate Lady.

There is a Canadian chocolate manufacturer that goes by that name. I thought it was odd that the "chocolate lady" was there, but later I learned that she was considered to be a Canadian hero and had saved many people's lives:

"It happened between the Canadians (or British) and the United States, at a time when the borders were first being established between the two countries. On June 21st, 1813 a group of American soldiers took over the home where Laura Secord and her husband lived, an area known as Queenston, Upper Canada. As her husband was recovering from a previous battle, he was unable to do anything about the "take over" and Laura was forced to take care of these intruders, cooking, cleaning and service them drinks. It was after overhearing the soldiers plans to attack the British side of the Niagara peninsula, that she decided to warn the British. She waited until the men fell asleep and then walked barefoot for 20 miles (32 km) to warn the British about the possible invasion. As a result, all but six of the soldiers were captured.

In a letter from Lieutenant James Fitzibbon he describes Laura Secord's heroic endeavour:

"The weather on the 22nd day of June, 1813 was very hot, and Mrs. Secord, whose person was slight and delicate, appeared to have been and no doubt was very much exhausted by the exertion she made in coming to me, and I have ever since held myself personally indebted to her for her conduct upon that occasion..."

The vision continued: *I seemed to have gone from an Egyptian experience to a Catholic one, which was very unusual, especially since my background was Jewish. What surprised me even more, was that these people knew me, and I seemed to know them! They were excited to show me where they lived. Once inside, I remember saying "I feel like I don't deserve to be here", and then someone said "Don't worry, you will". I couldn't possibly imagine what it was that I would do that would qualify me to live with saints!*

At that very moment I looked up and saw two white horses, spirits -- the most beautiful horses I had ever seen. They were flying in the sky towards me, and behind them, I could see "a city on a cloud". It wasn't as if I had any choice in the matter, because instantly I found myself in that city, recognizing it was the Heavenly version of Jerusalem. I had been to the physical one many years before, and it looked the very same, except that it was completely empty and had a "golden glow" about it. I found myself walking along the street known as the "Via Dolorosa" the same path that Jesus walked along as he carried the cross. I turned to the right and was greeted by two of the most amazing looking statues of lions, their manes gloriously peaked, and they appeared so regal. Then someone whispered in my ear that I would be going inside the Temple, and that I wouldn't be able to stay too long because the energy was so strong.

Upon entering, I remember the light being sooo brilliantly bright that it was "as if the Sun itself" was inside the temple. Through all of this brightness, my eyes could faintly see a "Being of Light" on a throne about the size of an apartment building! I remember thinking to myself "surely I wouldn't be allowed to see God, but whoever this is, it must be someone very close to Him". Either I passed out, or my memory was blocked, but after awhile, as I began to wake up, I heard myself saying "God, I love you". Not as if I was talking to God, but as if I was talking to my husband, someone I was in love with. As I opened my eyes, I realized that I had my head in this man's lap, and he had his hand on my cheek. As he gazed down at me, I could see that this man had shoulder length golden blonde hair, and the bluest eyes I had ever seen. I wondered to myself, who could this possibly be, that I seemed to be so "in love" with. At first I thought I must be dreaming about my husband when he was young." His hair used to be blonde, but he always wore it short, and his eyes had never appeared that blue to me before. As my eyes began to focus, I soon realized that this man had a very narrow nose, quite different from my husband's. I looked around to see where I was, noticing that we were in a very large hall with pillars. It looked like there had been some type of banquet or celebration. I kept wondering who this person was, this man whom I had told that I loved. Then he moved his hand away from my face and I noticed a huge scar in the palm of his hand. I realized who this was.

Chapter 29

"Magdalene"

Of course, I have wondered for years about the experience, and one day after sharing the "vision" with some friends, one of them suggested that perhaps I was Mary Magdalene in a past life. Of course when this had originally taken place, I didn't know anything about Mary Magdalene, except that she was considered to be a "prostitute" and that she had washed Jesus' feet with her hair. I had no idea that she had been married to Jesus. It was through my years of research, and of course with the release of Dan Brown's "DaVinci Code" that I learned of the possibility. Eventually I learned that right around the time I had that experience, during 1995, 1996, & 1997 many other women were also having similar dreams or visions. This was and is happening all over the world, and each of them believed that they to, were Mary Magdalene in a past life. They are called "the Magdalenes".

I had never before thought that I could be anyone quite so famous in a past life, but I have since learned that we can belong to "monads". A monad is our spiritual family, and many people that belong to the same monad, can have experiences that might lead them to believe that they were a particular person in a past life.

Over the years I met many people who are very psychic, and one of them told me that she believed I was "Isis" in a past life. I remember thinking at the time "I couldn't possibly have been anyone as important as that, and it would be very egotistical to even think so". Yet because of the experience I had with Isis in Petra, I felt so very "connected" to her, and to be quite honest, the possibility had crossed my mind. Yet other people were saying that because of my experience with Jesus, I may have been Mary Magdalene. It all seemed so strange, and impossible for me to believe at the time. But since I have learned about "monads" I began to believe that I possibly could belong to the same monad as Isis, and that perhaps Mary Magdalene is part of that monad as well. My friend Magi told me that she began thinking that she was Isis when she was still only a child, and my Reiki Master, Dorothy, had also thought she too had a past life as Isis.

Months later I had another dream in which I was in the south of France. I seemed to know exactly where I was, without being told, or seeing any signs, it was just a "knowing". I was climbing up the side of a riverbed towards a cave. I came upon a woman deep inside the cave who was dressed like a nun, wearing a black robe with a headpiece and a white ruffle above the forehead. She looked to be in her "sixties". She looked me straight in the eye and said "I am the Heart of the Sacred Heart". At the time, I was not familiar with the term "Sacred Heart" but had known of a "Catholic School" with that name. It seems that this is the name that Jesus is sometimes called, because of his deep love for humanity. Interestingly, the Tarot refers to "Hearts" as "Cups" which can also be "Grails" and this woman was telling me that she was the "Heart of the Sacred Heart" or the "Grail of the Holy Grail". Dan Brown in his book, expresses the idea that the words "Holy Grail" is a term used to describe the bloodline of Mary Magdalene. "Sangreal" the word from which Holy Grail is derived, has been interpreted San Greal; which means holy grail. However, it has also been suggested that Sangreal should be divided into the words Sang and Real meaning Royal Blood.

It was shortly after having this experience that someone loaned me a book called "The Lineage of the Codes of Light" by Jessie E. Ayani. It was while reading this book that I learned that Mary Magdalene used to meditate in a cave in the south of France, and where she may have spent her last years of life!

Of course, the synchronicity continues, and just as I finished editing this last chapter, I received in an email from a friend. It was a channeled message from Mary Magdalene, through Gillian MacBeth-Louthan, in which she addresses her "Daughters of the Heart, Daughters of the Grail", and Daughters of the Sun/Son, stating that we hold within us the "Holy Encodings" - a holy message for the world to hear, a message hidden within each of us who belong to the "Order of Magdalene" which is the "Order of the

Sacred Feminine". This confirmed my inclination about the heart and the grail.

In 2009 I began waking up in the middle of the night to write down the many messages I was receiving. The messages came to me as stories in the form of poetry, they would just flow through me, and were completed in a matter of minutes. It was about a dream I had a year prior - I was swimming with dolphins, thinking I was one as well, but then noticed that my upper body was human.

Gene-Isis

"La Mer" is the name of the sea that is laden

With maidens awaiting for thee

And the dolphins surrounded your self

As you mounted the waves

And the crests of the sea

You thought you were a dolphin

And you were "in a sense" you will see

For the name "dear one" - has a meaning that's laden

With a crown for a French King or Queen

"Mystic" - Rosaline Temple

And as you looked down - you enforced the power

Of the energy keeping you afloat

And a tail you did see, as well as we

Two breasts of a human being

So as you watched and kept afloat

It became obvious to you and to me

That you were not a human or a dolphin

But a "mermaid" of the sea

The name that is known of legends so old

Is that Mari means "of the Sea"

And stems from a vine that is blood of wine

And royalty "meant to be"

And so it is told, that the names of old

"Mari" and "vine of the King"

Is a mixture of both, that came to be known

As the "Merovingian line" of thee

For the blood of the vine, is that of wine

And is associated with "the grail"

For thy cup "runneth over" with blood of "the line"

And the "Mer" that is of the sea

For when Earth was created and the way that G-d made it

He surrounded her with water

It was during this time that our genetic line

Also came to be

So Isis and Mari, and Aphrodite

Were one and the same, you see

For each one of them is part of "creation"

And Gene-Isis began with the sea

And the "one" whose name – means "of the great line"

Which is made of "Magda" and "lene"

Is also the "one" who is of the lineage

And the "grail" that was "set out to sea"

"Mystic" - Rosaline Temple

For when they arrived, Martha and Mary

And the young one called Sara, as well

They were escorted by Joseph Arimathea

The one who "this story" did tell

For when they did flee from the shores where they dwelled

It was Egypt they set out to see

But after some time they soon decided

That France was the place they should be

And that would be where they would live

While He would watch over thee

So myths began and stories were told

To create "truths" that were spoken - but hidden

About the lineage that is our inheritance

And known as the "Merovingian"

.....Rosaline Temple

With the release of Dan Brown's book and the movie "The DaVinci Code" it became well known that Jesus and Mary Magdalene might have been married, and possibly had children. If you are not familiar with the "Merovingians" they are believed to be the bloodline of the children stemming from this illustrious couple. The early Royal House of France also appears to be linked to these so called "Long Haired Kings" of the Merovingian bloodline, who descended from a tribe in Germany, known as "The Franks". Referred to - as "Sorcerer Kings" these tall, blonde people ruled areas of Germany and France from the 5th to the 7th century.

Rumour has it, that the Merovingian Dynasty originates from very strange parenting, as the first so-called "Merovingian human being" was conceived from two fathers, one human, and the other supposedly "of the sea" - which gave the Merovingian magical qualities. They sometimes referred to this "sea being" as a "Quinotaur". These people were very adept in the healing arts, and they also had exceptionally strong ESP skills. The myth goes on to say that those of the "bloodline" had a birthmark that looked like a cross, which is supposed to be somewhere between the shoulders, or over the heart. It is also believed that this cross, linked them with the "Templars".

In the book "The Hiram Kay", the authors Christopher Knight and Robert Lomas state that within some "Merovingian" burial sites, they have discovered specific objects, which included tiny golden bees, a golden bull's head, and a crystal ball. But what has become the most eminent belief pertaining to this lineage, is that the Merovingians are supposedly descendants of Mary Magdalene and Jesus. I particularly found it interesting that a "crystal ball" was included in the discovery, as I had recently had a vision of Jesus in which he was showing me several different types of crystal balls, and instructing on how to use them for healing. At the time, I had thought it was strange that Jesus would be showing me crystals for healing. I have since learned that crystals are of great significance, as there is something within our DNA that connects with them, and also the earth, as her centre is a crystalline matrix.

Chapter 30

"The Scent of Roses"

It was after having the experience with Jesus that upon waking, I could smell roses everywhere. At first, I thought that my daughter had sprayed some perfume in the house, but she wasn't home, and the fragrance seemed to be following me around. In fact, the smell was so strong, that when I got into my car, I thought my husband had hidden one of those "deodorizers" somewhere in the car. I had to drive with my windows down because the smell was so strong!

I was going to a real estate meeting, and when I got there, I happened to be seated next to an East Indian gentleman. I hadn't seen him for several weeks, and he asked me how I was doing. I told him that I wasn't selling much real estate, but other than that, things were going quite well. I was really surprised when he said "Yes, I can see you've been doing a lot spiritually." I was totally stunned when he said that, and of course, I asked him how he could tell. He said "...by the light coming from your forehead. Not only that, someone is with you, and they are standing right behind you." At that moment, his cell phone rang, and he left the meeting, and that was the last time I actually ever saw him.

I never did find out who was with me, but when I left the meeting, I went over to Val's. I told her that I could smell roses everywhere, and she replied "Oh, that's Mother Mary!" When I went upstairs, I noticed that she had a photograph lying on her coffee table, which looked very much like the man I had seen in my vision, whom I believed to be Jesus. I couldn't understand how she could have a *photograph* of this person, especially if it was who I thought it was. I also wondered if I had seen it before, and perhaps it had triggered the experience. She confirmed my thoughts on who it was, and of course, I wanted to know how she could possibly have a "photograph" of Jesus, since cameras hadn't been invented when he supposedly lived on earth. Val said that she had been given the photo that very day, and then told me the story surrounding it.

She said that a couple from England took a photo of the "shroud of Turin". The shroud is a controversial item in itself. It is supposedly the fabric that Jesus had been wrapped in, after he had been taken down from the cross. (At that time, Jewish people would be wrapped in a cloth in preparation for burial.) This particular shroud has an image on it that looks like a "negative" of a photograph. It is believed that when Jesus was "resurrected" the light created an image onto the cloth he was wrapped in. The shroud has been kept by the church, and handed down through the centuries. It is presently kept in a museum in Italy, in the town of Turin. Many scientists over the years have conducted DNA and carbon testing to see if there is any truth to the claims.

Anyway, Val said that the couple took a photo of the "negative" image and brought it with them on their visit to see Sai Baba, the Avatar in India. They wanted to know if the image really was Jesus. Baba took the photo and a few days later, just before they were leaving to return home, he gave it back to them, wrapped in brown paper, saying "Yes, this was how Jesus looked when he walked upon the earth." When the couple returned home, they unwrapped the package and to their surprise the negative had been turned to a "positive" revealing an image of Jesus, with eyes open. This photo was *exactly* how I saw him in my vision. There was no doubt in my mind that this was the very same person I had seen.

That evening I was watching a documentary on TV about a church in France. They were saying that the original church had burnt down in a fire, but there was one object that was in the church, which didn't burn. It was a garment, believed to be worn by Mary, and it was the only thing that didn't burn. Since then, the Church has been rebuilt and was dedicated to Her, and they have the dress on display. It is called the "The Sancta". They said that when they rebuilt the church, "it was constructed to take advantage of the natural light" which gave a beautiful effect. I found the last sentence rather metaphoric, because the Rosicruscian's believe that "the Rose" is the Divine Feminine, but they also believe it represents "the Church".

As I watched the show about the church, I noticed that every once in a while, I could smell roses again. At first I didn't pay too much attention to it, but after awhile it became obvious that whenever Mary's name was mentioned, the fragrance became stronger. I also noticed that there was a symbol on the side of the church that looked very much like the one on my wristwatch. It was an "antique" styled watch, and the fragrance seemed to get stronger whenever they showed the symbol. I somehow felt that I was being shown a connection with the symbol, the rose, and time. The Church was "Chartres" a very famous church.

I had previously discovered that Roslin, the Edinburgh Chapel, was built on an area that was known as a Rose Line, a leyline, but didn't realize that the line traveled all the way down to the South of France, where there was a Tower built in honour of Mary Magdalene, called Rene Le Chateau. Several years later when Dan Brown's "The DaVinci Code" was published, I learned that this "rose line" was once considered to be the Prime Meridean of Paris – a time line. For some reason, I was being shown that there was a connection with the Divine Feminine, the Rose Line, and time. Of course, the "Rose Line" also represents the "lineage" or bloodline of Jesus and Mary Magdalene. The word "prime" means "of the highest importance" or the "earliest in time". After doing some research I discovered that there is a connection to "time" at Chartres Cathedral. There is a huge labyrinth inside the church, as well as a conspicuous paved "flagstone" that stands out from the all the rest. Every year on June 21st, at a particular time, a ray of sunlight shines through one of the windows onto that particular flagstone, and hundreds of people come to walk the labyrinth on that particular day. As well, there is a very famous window called the "rose window". Apparently this cathedral has drawn a lot of attention throughout history. It has attracted pilgrims for thousands of years and while it would be impossible to prove, rumour states that the cathedral was built on top of what previously was a Druid temple, built in honour of the one who they referred to as the "Virgo Paritura" (the virgin who will conceive).

Chapter 31

"Spider - Woman"

I had the feeling that I was at someone's funeral. Everyone was lined up, and each person was paying "respects" to a couple that were standing at the front. In the dream, I recall the woman asking me if I would be willing to participate in a ceremony which involved "shouting". It seemed like a strange request at the time, and I didn't quite understand what she wanted me to do. The man next to her said "I bet she won't have the guts to do it!" Of course, that's all he had to say, I knew instantly, that it didn't matter what it was, I would do it, just to spite his words!

In the next scene, I found myself walking along a path in the woods, and suddenly noticed that there was a giant- sized spider up ahead of me. In my "three-dimensional" life, I have always been terrified of spiders, and seeing this one in my dream state, wasn't any different, especially since this spider was probably the size of a house! But, something quite overwhelming happened. The spider was emanating the feelings of "love" that were so strong and powerful, that any fear that I had was completely vanished, and I myself seemed to be put into a pure state of love. Then I woke up.

It was the middle of the night, and as I was wide awake, I decided to do a bit of reading. I went to the bookshelf and picked out a book I had been reading called "Pyramid Energy: The Philosophy of God, the Science of Man, by Dean and Mary Hardy, and Marjorie Killick. Ever since my Egyptian experiences, I was fascinated with anything that had to do with Egypt. In fact, I couldn't get enough information. So I picked up the book, and just randomly opened it. I was quite amazed, once again, when I looked down to see that the chapter I had selected was "the Legend of Spider Woman".

In many of the traditional stories passed down among the Native Americans, Spider Woman is considered to be a great teacher, a wisdom keeper, and protector. She is sometimes referred to as Grandmother Spider, the woman who, *through her dreams*, created the earth as well as humanity. She represents energy and the power of creativity. She weaves a web of knowledge, through her geometric shapes, connecting all, including past, present and future.

According to the Hopi Legend, Spider Woman came into "being" when the First World was created. She was to remain on the earth as the "Creator's" helper. She was given the power to help create life. She was given the knowledge, the wisdom, and the love to bless all the beings she created.

Following the Creator's instructions, Spider Woman took some earth and mixed it with some saliva and molded it into two beings, twins.

Each of the twins was created to help keep the world in order by sound and touch.

Each of the twins traveled all over the world fulfilling their duty. The first twin traveled all around the world placing his hands upon the earth, so that it would become solidified. The second twin traveled all of the earth, sounding or shouting out his call as he was told to do. He made the whole world an instrument of sound, an instrument for carrying messages, resounding praise to the Creator of all. "These will be your duties in time to come," said Spider Woman.

She then created all of the plant-life, including flowers and trees, birds and animals. "It is very good," said the Creator, happily. "It is now ready for human life, the final touch to complete my plan."

According to the story told in the "Pyramid" book, the twin who was in charge of sound, eventually struck a bad chord, which caused "chaos" on the earth. Because of this, Spider Woman had the people of the earth build medicine wheels at specific times and places, in order to bring harmony and balance to the earth.

After reading the story, I thought about my dream. Someone was dying, and I was being asked to perform a type of ceremony, and shout! I knew that it had something to do with "the land". It was fall, and the leaves were dying. I wondered if this was what the "funeral" represented. I felt compelled to gather some of my friends together and go to a specific place, to perform a ceremony. I called several, and we looked on the calendar, noticing that it was almost

September 22nd, Fall Equinox. We decided to get together on that particular day.

I asked everyone to bring drums or any instruments that they had, and we met in the parking lot of Campbell Valley Park, in Langley, BC. I wasn't sure why, but that was the place that I thought we were supposed to have the ceremony. We began walking along a path, and then I suddenly felt the urge to go into a meadow that was just filled with colourful flowers that came all the way up to our shoulders. As we walked amongst them, one of my friends said she felt as if we were taking part in the movie called "What Dreams May Come" – in the scene where they were also walking through a field of beautiful flowers. It seemed ironic that she said that, as we were doing just that. "Doing something that had come from a dream."

We formed a circle and walked in "geometrical" patterns, drumming and shouting, and I'm sure that if anyone had seen us, they would have thought we were out of our minds. A group of grown women behaving like children. But we did it, and we had a great time doing it. When we had finished, we sat down, and had lunch. As we sat there, suddenly one woman looked over my shoulder and pointed to a cloud saying "Look, that cloud looks exactly like a spider!" When I looked up, I was truly in a state of shock. I had previously told each of them that I had been "guided" to do this, but hadn't told any of them specific details about the dream. I immediately shared it with them, and we were all amazed that this could happen! I truly felt that "Spider Woman" was showing herself to us, in acknowledgement for performing the ceremony. I began to realize that I had some type of connection with the Earth.

Chapter 32

"The Universal Flower Language"

After performing the ceremony for Spider Woman, and receiving "confirmation" from beyond the veil, I realized that this information needed to be shared.

I recalled that when I had asked "upstairs" what my purpose was, I had been told "The Universal Flower Language". My friend Dawn thought that it must have something to do with the "Flower of Life" teachings. I had been wondering for quite some time what exactly was expected of me, but suddenly came to the realization of what that was.

Ever since this all began, I had become very interested in the "healing arts" and whenever I had wanted to learn anything pertaining to that, a teacher would suddenly appear. Over the years, I learned how to "cleanse auras", work with sound, and crystals. I also learned the ancient art of Japanese healing and became a "Reiki Master". I was able to teach this to others, but I somehow knew deep in my heart, that this wasn't my "true" purpose.

I knew that Drunvalo Melchizadek was teaching a meditation called "The Flower of Life". But I had never taken his course. From speaking to others, I learned that the meditation I had been practicing was completely different, and I was having pretty good results. I also believed that the name "Universal Flower Language" implied that this teaching had something to do with "sacred knowledge" as over the centuries flowers have been used as symbols of enlightenment. I also sensed that it had something to do with the "meridians of the body" and the "leylines of the earth". ("Information passed down the generations" and "rose lines" as the name Rosaline implied.)

I decided to create a workshop, consisting of a combination of methods. It would be one evening, and two full days. The first evening I would share some of my dreams and visions, and then perform a "ceremony of remembrance". The second day would consist of sacred geometry and specific signs and symbols, among other things. In the afternoon we would concentrate on "energy work" based on the information given in the morning, as well as specific hand movements. On the third day, we would perform a ceremony outdoors.

I drew a symbol that looked both "Egyptian and Celtic" based on a symbol I had seen in a dream, and used it on the brochure. It was the head of an Egyptian Goddess with two exotic looking birds on either side, a triangle surrounding them, with a Celtic design for the background. At the time that I drew it, I didn't realize that it was bringing together the two places that I had been drawn to through my dreams and visions, Egypt and Scotland. I felt that whoever was drawn to the image, might be drawn to the teaching, which turned out to be true.

I had nine women who wanted to attend. I was really excited, but a little nervous. As well, I hadn't found a place where we would perform the "outdoor" ceremony. I remember meeting a couple of friends for lunch, and I was mentioning this. One of them asked me if I had been shown any places in my dreams. I recalled that I had, but the dream was so crazy, that I didn't think that it meant anything. It was actually quite a funny dream.

In it, someone had told me that I should go to "Bear Creek Park" to clean my sheets. (This was a public park in the area that I lived.) I hadn't been there in a number of years. I remember thinking in the dream that it was a strange place to have our sheets cleaned, as there wasn't a laundry place in the park.

Anyway, I took some sheets and put them in my car and went to the park. I noticed that my friend Margo, was standing at a door that led to a room hidden "underground". She had her arms loaded with gifts. I asked her if she was here to get her sheets cleaned, and she said that she was. I asked her what the gifts were for, and she said "they did such a good job the last time, that she was bringing them gifts". Just then the door opened, and we went inside. We sat down on some benches and I noticed there were a lot of men, also seated along the benches.

As we sat there, someone came over and handed each of us a "Menorah" a seven branched candleholder. Then Margo whispered in my ear "I hope the guy I get is handsome." Just then, I realized that "getting our sheets cleaned" wasn't exactly what I thought it meant! I got up to leave, and just as I did, a man jumped up wanting to purchase my Menorah for $88.00. I couldn't recall if I sold it to him or not.

When I went to the parking lot, I ran into one of my "high school" friends, a woman who was also about to leave. I noticed that she was carrying some sheets. I said to her, "Oh, did you get your sheets cleaned? She said " yes, he did a good job, but the guy was really ugly!"

Of course, you can imagine, we were all having quite a laugh at this dream, but one of the girls was a little surprised, as she thought it pertained to her. She was from Hawaii and taught "Tantra", a metaphysical teaching that was based on the sexual energy of the Kundalini. She said that she worked with couples, and in her workshop, each couple are supposed to bring sheets as well as gifts for each other, one for each of the chakras of the body. I recalled that I had once been shown that the "menorah" is a representation of our chakras. She said that she had studied under a woman whose first name just happened to be "Margo". She was amazed that I had this dream.

Anyway, after sharing the dream, everyone thought that I should check out "Bear Creek Park" to see if there was a place where we could have a ceremony, or (get our sheets cleaned).

That afternoon, I went to the park. I didn't use the front entrance, as I was familiar with the area and knew that it would be too wide-open, and there wouldn't be any privacy. I drove around to the other side and parked my car. I saw a sign saying "Bear Creek Flower Garden". Since my workshop was called "The Universal Flower Language" I decided to go into that area. I noticed that there was a grove of trees to my right, and headed in that direction, looking for "signs from the universe".

Of course, the workshop was based on an ancient Egyptian teaching, so I didn't expect to see anything of that nature, but after walking a few metres, I can honestly say, I could hardly believe my eyes. I'm sure that I must have had a "stunned" look on my face, as I stood there gazing at a statue of a Sphinx. Who would have believed that something so Egyptian would be right in the middle of Bear Creek Park? But there it was. As I came out of my hypnotic state, I remembered that a Sphinx is generally placed in front of a temple, and so I checked out the wooded area behind. Sure enough, it was large enough and the woods created privacy for us to create a "spiritual temple" and perform our ceremony. I had been guided to a place through a dream once again, and the Sphinx confirmed to me that I was in the right place!

A few days before the workshop, I met a couple of women who lived in my area. They were guests at a "gathering" I attended. There were about twelve of us, and we were practicing "psychometry". We sat in a circle, and each of us placed an item we owned into a bag. Most of the people placed a ring, or pendant, a special coin, or a stone, etc. Then we each selected an item out of the bag and placed it against our foreheads. We each took turns sharing any information that could "pick up". The item that I selected turned out to be a small green stone. I placed it on my forehead, and immediately was shown a circle with a cross inside. I somehow felt that this person was very balanced, into the healing arts, and worked with numbers and symbols. I also sensed that the person didn't work with individuals, but gatherings of a much larger scale. It turned out that this stone belonged to a woman who was a scientist, specializing in teaching officers in the military, the metaphysical aspects of equations, etc. She said that the symbol I saw was one that she worked with all the time. She was quite impressed with my "intuition" and wanted us to get together. She was staying at her friend's place, which turned out to be right around the corner from where I lived.

We met the next day, and I spent the afternoon visiting with the two of them. Each of these women were excited about the fact that I was going to be giving my very first "workshop" and both of them ended up contributing something toward it. Bonieta, the scientist, showed me a specific pattern that was to be used with crystal points, in a way similar to acupuncture, but done in specific areas of the head, and used during an "initiation". Donna had received a message about water. I can't remember the exact word, as it was very technical, but she had been given it in a meditation. When she looked it up, she said that the word described a formation of water molecules that gather together in the form of a "pentagram" – a Star of David. This can be created through a specific process. She realized that the Star of David was one of the symbols of the "Flower of Life" and she knew how to duplicate the process. She was kind enough to do this, and brought it over to me as a gift to use during the workshop. As they both worked with "flower essences" they also taught me how to create a "sacred flower essence" in time for the workshop, as well. They both would have come to the workshop, but Bonieta was flying back to California the following day, and Donna had already made plans to go away for the week-end.

It seemed that the universe was "pulling everything together for me". The first group of women attended Friday evening. They were really excited about all that transpired, and I could tell that they were really anxious to return the next day.

That evening, in the middle of the night I received a message. I heard a voice saying the words "Hashmal-Alhim, Hashmalhim". The words were truly a special gift.

"Hashmal" is a Hebrew word that means "Light Manifestation" and "to speak silently". A "Hashmal" is an Angel belonging to the "Order of Hashmalhim". This word can also describe a state of consciousness. Although they are Angels, they are the essence of the Language of Light. I hadn't realized that the "Hebrew Flaming Letters" I had received before, were actually Angels.

I learned that these particular Angels bring to us our blessings and gifts that we can receive through dreams, meditation, prayer and invocation, and they represent G-d silently answering our prayers. This was very synchronistic, because that morning, the workshop was composed of meditation and prayer, as well as sacred symbols. It is through these Angels that we can experience the Divine Light and an experience with God". They can attune the "energy gateways of our bodies", our chakras, and they also have the ability to repair and restructure them, to support new intelligence.

The word "Alhim" means "Infinitismal Particles of Spiritual Light". These particles are used to create a powerful "energy signal" for healing work, communication, and to spiritual gifts with the Masters of Light. In receiving this light, we experience "enlightenment" or a state of "gnosticism" a state of knowing. "Hashmalhim" is the word used for truly, higher states of consciousness. They are also protectors of the "laws of the universe". This was also very interesting, because the afternoon portion of the course, was about healing, working with the "Chakras" of the body, and receiving our sacred gifts from God. I was quite honoured that these Angels were blessing us with their presence. They showed me a particular hand movement to use, when doing the "energy work".

On the third day, we went to Bear Creek Park for the ceremony. Everyone seemed to have really enjoyed each day of the workshop, and gave me excellent feedback. I was pleased.

Chapter 33

"Earth Chakras"

Over the years, I was guided through my dreams and visions to go to various areas to perform ceremonies. Wherever I went I would be shown a sign of "confirmation" that I was in the right place, and the universe acknowledged what I was doing. It didn't matter how many times this happened, I was astonished each and every time.

At one point, a friend took me to a place that I hadn't visited before, Tynehead Park. She was surprised that I hadn't been there before, as I lived so close to the area. There were many beautiful walking trails throughout the park, with a hidden creek within the very centre. My friend brought some peanuts and bird seed with her, and I was thrilled to see that the squirrels weren't afraid to approach us, and that the birds would eat right out of our hands. It felt like this was how it must have been in the "original" garden, and how it "should be". I had lived in the area for many years, and hadn't realized that this beautiful place existed. I felt as if I had "missed out". We eventually came across a "butterfly garden" that was just beginning to bloom, and we stood there watching the show of winged creatures as they arrived. Butterflies are about transformation.

As we returned to the car, the energy of the place had an overwhelming affect on me, and I kept thinking that we should have a ceremony there, in the garden. As we walked along, the thought also suddenly occurred to me, that perhaps each of these places, all the ones I had been "led to" through my dreams, were power points - "earth chakras". Of course, I wasn't exactly sure. I knew that butterflies are sometimes used to represent the "third chakra" - the area around our stomach, the "solarplexus" the very place where we get "butterflies" when we are nervous. I remember asking Spirit "if this is true, and if this is a "chakra" then please show me a sign".

I went home and got ready for work. I was no longer selling cosmetics, but was working afternoons in a beautiful metaphysical bookstore giving "card readings" to their customers. The store was decorated to represent "heaven on earth" and the woman who owned the shop, was a window designer. She was able to recreate the shop into the most magical looking place, and everyone who came through the door was impressed. There were interesting items displayed throughout the store, and on that particular day, when I walked through the door, the counter was covered in a blanket of butterflies, that she had just unpacked. I had received "confirmation". The park *was* part of a chakra system, and the "butterfly garden" was the "solarplex". I was very excited when I realized this.

I began thinking about the different dreams I had and the places I was led to. In one of my very first dreams, I was shown "elephants dancing along a path" which I recognized as the area known as "Mud Bay". I had been told to create a "temple" there called "The Temple of Sun Yin" meaning Male/Female. I was being asked to "balance" the energies of that particular place. I invited a friend, and we went down to the "bay" to see where the best area would be to do this. I asked to be shown "a sign" and a cloud took the shape of a "Ram" just above a grove of trees, one of two places we had been considering. We created a brochure, inviting any and all "who felt drawn to come" and on the night of the ceremony, people showed up from all over the mainland. A "Blue Heron" circled above us, the whole evening, which was of great significance to me, as it is our North American version of the Egyptian Ibis, whom I associate with the Egyptian Scribe, Thoth. I felt that the bird's presence was a "confirmation" from nature, that our "ceremony" was acknowledged.

I found a book about Chakras, and began looking for the symbols associated with each one. I learned that the word Chakra, means "spinning wheel" and comes from the ancient language of India, known as Sanskrit. These are major centres located throughout the body, as well as the earth, which balance energy. Some people who are able to "see auras" can actually see these "wheels" in our bodies. The first chakra is usually called "the root" or "base". I searched through the book, and sure enough, there was an "Elephant" associated with this particular chakra, just as I had been shown in my dream. The article said that the elephant's trunk represents "the serpent" which sits at the base of the spine and climbs upward. What I found amazing is that "Mud Bay" - the area where we were guided to perform the ceremony, is the mouth of a river called the "Serpentine". How amazing is that?

In the dream about "Bear Creek Park" I had been shown sheets and gifts, as well as "menorah's, which represent our chakras, but the overall dream had a sexual theme. If you study the second chakra, you will find that it is referred to as the "sacral" or "sexual chakra". It is situated approximately two inches from the belly button, in the area of the womb. Although it is often seen symbolized with a fish, I associate it with the "Bear" as this was what I had been shown. I have since been guided to several other areas that are "sacral chakras" and they always show me a "Bear" in the vision, and one appears in one form or another at the location. I thought it was pretty clever of my guides, since the womb is the place where you "bear" children.

All this time, my guides had been showing me a specific line of "chakras" within the area I lived. Of course, this system was only one of the many all over the world, as there are systems within systems, and each are part of a greater one, encompassing the whole earth.

I soon learned to trust what I was being shown. Even if it seemed completely crazy, I would make an effort to find the place, and was never disappointed. For example, in one dream I was shown a fully decorated Christmas Tree, which was at some sort of entrance, that they wanted me to find it. When I woke up, I laughed, because it was the end of February, but I figured that even if I couldn't find the tree, it would still be a nice drive. I called a friend and we ventured out on a search. I couldn't recall the whole dream, but I somehow knew that this was about the "throat chakra" and I "sensed" that it was in an area known as Fort Langley. As we drove along I shared my dream, and of course she laughed, saying "we might find some kind of Christmas tree, but I doubt if it will be decorated!" As we drove up and around, we came upon a road called "Telegraph Trail" and since the throat chakra has to do with "communication" I thought we should follow the road. We had only driven a few miles, when suddenly she started pointing. She was so excited that she could hardly speak. There it was "a Christmas tree, completely decorated with silver and gold balls, and large red ribbons" at the end of February. It was right at the entrance to a place that sold Evergreen Trees and I guess the decorated tree was their "calling card". The two of us could hardly believe it. I now associate Christmas Trees with the fifth chakra, because of the dream.

I began reading everything I could about leylines and power points. In the book "The Light Shall Set you Free" by Norma J. Milanovitch and Shirley D. McCune, the authors state that during the time of Atlantis, there were crystals placed inside the earth, as well as the "etheric" bodies of the Priests and Priestesses. It was their "duty" to walk along these pathways allowing the crystals within their bodies to interact with those of the earth. It was considered one of the greatest honours to do this! When I read those words, I felt deeply moved that I had been given this gift.

Chapter 34

"Tequila Minerva"

It was sometime around 1998 when my mom, who was in her seventies at the time was at a dance with my sister and brother-in-law, and myself. It was a "big band dance" and we were helping the woman who puts on the dances, who was a good friend of our mom's. While there, the heel on my left shoe suddenly broke. I was a little freaked out, because the left side of the body represents the feminine side, and the heel supports you. The only female I knew that was very supportive of me was my mother, not physically, but mentally, and I hoped that nothing was wrong with her. It was within minutes that my sister came over to tell me that mom wasn't doing very well, and that we should take her home.

When we got to her place, I put on a pair of my mom's slippers, and only had them on a few minutes, when the soul began to separate from the rest of the shoe. My sister looked at me and I could tell by the look on her face, that she was upset. "What do you think that means?" she said. I became frightened, and told her that I hoped our mother's soul wasn't thinking about leaving. Anyways, we thought that mom would feel better once she was home, but unfortunately, she seemed to get worse, and we ended up calling an ambulance. They took her to the hospital, and ended up admitting her, saying that she would be staying for a few days, while they checked things out. We were quite concerned.

Right around that same time, my son was looking for work. He had recently moved to California, and his girlfriend had a job, but he hadn't found one yet. As I crawled into bed, I began praying for my mother to become well, and for my son to find a job.

I had the following dream.

My mother and I were sitting on a park bench in an amusement park. Suddenly, I noticed that my mother, was no longer sitting next to me. When I looked up, I was shocked to see her swinging on a trapeze. I recall feeling horrified, especially when she stood up and let go with her hands, while the trapeze was swinging! As dreams go, she was on the ground in a flash, and as she came towards me she said "they call me Tequila Minerva. Next time I'm going to ask for more money."

I woke up laughing while at the same time wondering about the dream. I didn't sense that this had anything to do with chakras, or that I was supposed to look for a particular park. That evening, I attended another metaphysical gathering, with the same group of people. This time we were studying cards. Someone brought a deck and handed each one of us a card. When I looked at my card, I almost fell over, as there was a "woman on a trapeze" with the word "wholeness" underneath. I knew that my mom would be alright.

The next day, I went to the hospital to pick up my mom. When I arrived, she informed me that we were going out for lunch with a couple of her friends, and went to a Greek restaurant. As we finished eating, she said that she had to go next door to get some type of "special" drink that they only carried at that particular place. I told her that I would pay the bill and then meet her there. She said ok, I'll see you in Minerva's. I was so surprised, because that was the name she mentioned in the dream "Tequila Minerva". I remembered that my dad had used that phrase in a joke "to-kill-a-my-nerve-a" but it meant "to stop being nervous". But I thought it was funny, because now two items from my dream came to fruition.

That very same evening, my son called. He was really excited because he had a job offer. He said that he wasn't sure if he should take the offer, or counter for more money. I asked him what the name of the company was, and he said "Trapezio" - I was stunned once again, with the insightfulness of my dream. Of course, I shared it with him, and he said "Well, I guess I'll just accept the job, and NEXT time ask for more money, which is what he did."

I got off the phone, and went to the computer to look up the company's website. I noticed at the bottom written in small print, it said that the company was owned by "Athena Corp". I decided to look up the Goddess Athena, and discovered that she was a Roman Goddess, but in Greece she was often referred to as Minerva! She was known as the Goddess of Wisdom, Art and Knowledge. She was the companion of heroes, and it was in her honour, that the city of Athens was named, and the Parthenon built.

Eventually the company was sold and is no longer a software company, but my son has continued to have success in his career. I was truly overwhelmed with the information brought through in my dreams, and the Goddess was definitely showing her presence and helping my family. I was truly thankful to her and to God.

Chapter 35

"The Sixth Day"

The ancient Vedic scriptures declare that "the physical world operates under one fundamental law of maya (illusion)." - Paramahansa Yogananda.

As I read those words, I suddenly received an email, which said "Escape the Illusion!" I couldn't help but laugh. It was an article written about The Sixth Day of the Mayan Calendar, which was November 13th, 2008, and the very day it was sent to me. It seemed very synchronistic, and I couldn't help but wonder if there was a connection between the Mayan and Hindu teachings.

The Maya were incredible timekeepers, being able to predict amazing events. They created several calendars, one of these is known as "the Tzolkin". According to this calendar, we have now entered a very special time, which I felt was very significant as it was only days since the United States had elected Barack Obama as their 44th President. The Sixth Day represents a time of awakening and enlightenment. Just as the petals of a lotus blossom begin to unfold, a time of unconditional love descends upon us. It represents the 11th of the 13 Heavens of the Galactic Cycle, and a new era of Heavenly Light.

As the Fifth Night fades into our past, and we enter this time of enlightenment, we will eliminate from our lives what no longer serves us, and we will begin to understand that we each have a specific purpose and a mission to fulfill. We will evolve into more spiritual beings, realizing that we have a connection with the earth, and everything around us. More and more of us will begin to remember the ancient ceremonies of the past, and answer the call that is put forth to us as we awaken to the new energy.

It was believed by many that Barack Obama would act as a catalyst in bringing this "new era" to fruition, as his name signifies. In an excerpt from Gordon Davidson and Corinne McLaughlin's special edition of "Spiritual Dimensions of Obama's Leadership" they stated that his name means:

"A good and handsome man, carrying spiritual wisdom and blessings from G-d – empowering wholeness and balance as father and mother, or masculine and feminine energies."

The name Barack stems from the African word "baraka" which means blessing, and in the Semitic languages "spiritual wisdom" or "a blessing transmitted from God." The "O" in Obama is a symbol of wholeness or completion. "Ba" in Arabic means father and of course "ma" means mother. Hussein, his middle name, in Arabic means "good, or good looking."

As the elections came to a close, the United States and world monetary systems began to collapse, and we were shown that the old system was not working anymore, and as the Sixth Day implies "we will eliminate from our lives what no longer serves us". As Obama's campaign slogan implied "it is time for change" and according to the Sixth Day "change is upon us". As you are aware, Obama won the first election, and as I edit this material, January, 2012 he is preparing to run for a second time. His slogan "it's time for change" was certainly true, but as it turned out, he was unable, during this first term, to achieve this goal. 2011 turned out to be a year of political upheaveal, earthquakes, tsunamis, riots and economic chaos. Although it appeared that this man's heart was in the right place, Congress did not seem to agree with his wishes, and as a result, he was unable to move forward with many of his original ideas. People were still unemployed, and losing their homes, there was political unrest, and many were taking to the streets protesting. Change was upon us, and it was showing up all over the world, especially in the Middle East, where many countries began overthrowing their dictatorship governments, in hopes of forming one more democratic.

In the past few years, we have seen influential people in corporations, government and the church, involved in sex scandals, the misuse of power and money, and especially the misuse in controlling our natural resources. This was all part of the evening of the Fifth Night, but as the wheel turns, and the time of transition is upon us, many of these individuals have fallen and will continue to fall from their ivory towers as their greediness and misuse of power is exposed to the world. As the truth is revealed, they will continue to appear undignified in the eyes of the public, and where others would feel guilt and ashamed of what they have done, they appear without remorse, unaffected by their actions.

As we move into the morning of the Sixth Day, we will discard the old making room for the new. Simone Butler in her article entitled: "Winds of Change" states that "the chaos that will reign through the two-year period of the Sixth Day and Night is necessary for the creation of an enlightened world. The Golden Age can only emerge out of a series of transformative pulses, including periods of destruction. The very process that breaks down the world economic and political hierarchy also paves the way for a new world to flower."

In order to move into a higher level of consciousness, we must learn how to raise our vibrations, which can only be accomplished by being loving and compassionate beings. We must learn to choose the path of love over fear. We must learn to make the right choices, choices that will create a better world to live in. Each of us must become more aware of the decisions that we make, and the consequences that will occur by making them. We must learn to follow our intuition, and realize that as a stone thrown into a pond makes waves, for every action there is a reaction. That each and every thought, word or action we take has an impact on the universe. We are here for a reason, we all have an important role to play and it is part of our sacred contract.

Chapter 36

"Divine Government"

Christmas Eve, 2008. My husband and I went to Vancouver for the holidays to spend Christmas and Chanukah with our family. We had an unusual amount of snow and while we got to spend some time with family, we ended up being "snowed in" on Christmas Eve, and had to cancel our plans. Our evening wasn't very eventful, and we sat around watching TV with my brother-in-law. But later on in the evening something very strange happened. I was watching Sylvia Browne, on the Montel William show, and while she was talking to someone, right when she said the word "angel" the television screen suddenly went black and all I could hear was static, and then along the bottom of the screen I read the following: On February 27th the full ..... and then the show came back on. I wondered if anyone else saw it, and what would happen on February 27th? Would there be a full moon on that day? I checked it out, and there wasn't, so when I got home I decided to "google" the words "Angelic Message February 27th" and up popped a list of websites, with this one at the top: "innerjourneyministries.org/angelic messages.html". After clicking onto it, I read the words

"This page is to share with you the many Angelic Messages I have received over the past few months in email. There are many things going on in our Universe and Spirit wants everyone to know. Each message has been channeled through someone. These messages will be posted by date completed including the name of the person who channeled them and anything that came with the email. G-d Speed you on your path, Namaste "

I scanned down the page to see if there was a message for February 27th, sure enough there was. It had been transmitted in 2002, which I refer to as the "year of the heart". The reason I call it that, is because if you break it down numerically, 2002 becomes the number 22, a master number. If you turn the left "2" around, the two "2's" together form a heart. The article was titled "Light Writings #13" and 13 represents Love - and the "Divine Feminine" in Hebrew. The heart is the shape that represents "love" therefore I felt that the message was coming from the "Sacred Heart".

It was an article written by Patricia Diane Cota-Robles, and amazingly she gave permission for the article to be reproduced in any form at all. Her message was so "encompassing" of everything that was in my heart that I felt it was important for everyone to read, and I surely couldn't have expressed it better myself. After being led to the article from a message on the television, you can imagine my surprise when I read the first line, which said: *"Communication networks around the world are being flooded with valid information"....*

Although the article was transmitted in 2002, I have come to believe that "a message is received" when the time is right for us to hear or read it. Interestingly, the article was a "clarion call" for lightworkers to gather and create a Chalice of Light to activate the Matrix and Archetype for Divine Government in the physical world of form. This meeting took place in August of 2002. I wasn't aware of the meeting at that time, but I know from other experiences, that "those of us" who are part of this amazing plan that she writes about, and who may not have been there physically, possibly did take part spiritually, even though we may not remember or be aware of the experience. I couldn't help but wonder who would be the one to fulfill this important role that she spoke about.

Here is the article:

We Still Have Time…. If We Act Now

by Patricia Diane Cota- Robles

Communication networks around the world are being flooded with valid information, misinformation and disinformation." During this unprecedented time, it is imperative that you, as a dedicated Lightworker, use your full capacity of Divine, Discerning Intelligence to evaluate everything that comes across your path. Take whatever you see, hear, read or experience into the deepest recesses of your heart, and blaze the Flame of Illumined Truth through it. Then command your manipulative, lower human ego into the Light, and ask your G-d Self to reveal to you any Truth that is contained within the information or message you received. Ask for everything that is not Truth to be clearly exposed to you as well. We have each been preparing for aeons of time to be the Heart, Head and Hands of G-d in the world of form during the defining moment of Earth's Transfiguration and Ascension. This is that moment!

It is vital that we stay on purpose and not get misled by the myriad distractions that are being projected onto the screen of life by the forces of imbalance. Any of the scenarios that indicate the "plan" is for someone else to miraculously intervene in our lives and save us in spite of ourselves and our free will is deception. It is true that we are receiving more assistance from the Legions of Light in the Heavenly Realms than ever before, but we are responsible for co-creating the perfection of Heaven on Earth ourselves.

Each of us alone must make the personal decision as to whether or not we are going to voluntarily do what is necessary in order to Ascend up the Spiral of Evolution with the planet Earth and the rest of Humanity. No one outside of ourselves can do that for us. Our G-d Selves know this. That is exactly why we agreed to go through countless lifetimes of preparation in order to be capable of fulfilling the mission we have embarked upon in this lifetime. We are co-creating, with the assistance of the entire Company of Heaven, a unique experiment that has never been attempted in any system of worlds.

Never, in the whole of creation, has a planet that has fallen to this depth of negativity and chaos been given the opportunity to Ascend through two dimensional shifts in such a short period of time. We are Ascending up the Spiral of Evolution from the 3rd Dimension through the 4th Dimension into the 5th Dimension. The reason the prophets and seers of ancient times foretold of the coming Golden Age of Eternal Peace and Prosperity is because they witnessed what life on Earth will be like in the 5th Dimensional Realms of Limitless Physical Perfection. The 5th Dimension vibrates with a frequency of Light that transcends the discord and maladies we are experiencing on Earth. The mutated frequencies of disease, poverty, war, corruption, greed, hatred, suffering, pain, violence, death as we know it and every other human mis-creation cannot be sustained in the 5th Dimension.

That does not mean that every human being will Ascend into the 5th Dimension and miraculously start behaving in a positive way. What it means is that anyone who is not vibrating at a frequency of Light that is compatible with the 5th Dimension WILL NOT BE ABLE TO MAKE THE SHIFT. The souls who are refusing to accept the opportunity to move into the Light that is now being presented to every man, woman and child evolving on Earth will be left behind. They will be forced to continue their dysfunctional existence in a 3rd-Dimensional reality. That means for those unfortunate human beings the tragic plight of the most negative situations on the planet will continue. There will be no respite, and they will wallow in their misery and pain until a distant time in the future when they will once again be given the opportunity to awaken and move into the Light.

At the present time there are horrific things taking place all over the world, and yet there are millions of awakening Lightworkers who are working diligently with the Light to heal the pain and make things better. Can you even fathom what life will be like in the 3rd Dimension once the Lightworkers have completed their Ascension into the 5th Dimension, and only souls who are committed to wreaking havoc, pain and suffering are left behind? The thought of it breaks my heart and boggles my mind. When we witness the terrible pain and suffering people are inflicting on other people, the nature kingdom and the environment, it is difficult for us not to fall into the self-righteous attitude of thinking they deserve whatever they get. There may even be a lurking sense of gratification in imagining them writhing in agony in the 3ʳᵈ Dimension for what they have done. The only reason there is any comfort in those thoughts is because we have forgotten that we are all one, and those wayward souls are just other facets of ourselves. What affects one part of life affects all life. There is no separation.

Just for a moment, imagine that the most degenerate, evil person on the planet is someone you love. What if it is your child or your husband, wife or parent? Imagine how hard it would be for you to know they were suffering in poverty, war, oppression, disease, corruption, pain and all manner of human depravity while you are abiding in the wondrous 5ᵗʰ Dimensional Realms of Limitless Physical Perfection.

You understand that they have done horrible things, but in your heart of hearts you know that in spite of their appalling behavior, there is a person inside whom you love, a person whom you know is capable of better things. You believe, with every fibre of your being, that this person will one day awaken and choose to move into the Light. You never give up hope, and you keep holding the vision, invoking the Light and praying daily and hourly that they will wake up and choose to turn their life around in time to make the shift into the 5ᵗʰ Dimension. The feelings of love, compassion and hope you would have for a loved one in that situation are the same feelings the Spiritual Hierarchy is urgently striving to awaken within our hearts for ALL Humanity. It is only through our love, compassion and dedicated invocations of the Light that the recalcitrant souls who are resisting their own awakening have a chance to get their heads above the human effluvia of their lives in time to choose the path of Light.

We never know what set of circumstances compels people to choose the negative paths they have chosen or what causes them to make the self-destructive decisions they make. What we do know is that everybody is doing the best they can, according to their wisdom and understanding. That profound Truth was made very clear to me when I witnessed a documentary on television that included an interview with some six and seven year old Palestinian boys. These beautiful, normally innocent children were being brainwashed into being suicide bombers. Their eyes glistened with expectation as they reported that they could not wait until they were old enough to be suicide bombers. They said that the greatest honor they could give to Allah (God) was to give their lives to destroy Israelis. We hear the adult suicide bombers echoing the exact same corrupt beliefs. This is something they have been programmed to believe since they first formed rational thought. Mind control and negative programming is behind all of the maladies manifesting on Earth at this time. Whether people are programmed by their parents, teachers, peers, religions, governments, or life circumstances, destructive beliefs are taught; they are not inherent in the human psyche.

The belief that in order for us to survive and live in security, comfort and abundance we must compete with and often harm another part of life is an erroneous, fear-based program that has been instilled in the consciousness of the masses of Humanity for thousands of years. That negative belief system is self-perpetuating and manifests circumstances to confirm its validity. It is a self-fulfilling prophecy. That core belief is at the root of the atrocities we are now witnessing on the planet. Those atrocities include the looking-out-for-number one, dog-eat-dog consciousness associated with corporate corruption, the greed that is creating the collapse of the global economy, the disregard for the Earth that is resulting in environmental pollution, the abuse of power that is corrupting governments, the lack of reverence for life involved in wars, crimes, illegal drugs, gangs, violence, ethnic cleansing, prejudice, religious fanaticism, hatred, selfishness and one and on ad infinitum. It is now time for the collective of human consciousness that has sustained that fear-based belief for thousands of years to be shattered. It is time for a new Matrix and Archetype to be created in its place that will bathe the consciousness of the masses of Humanity with the patterns of perfection from the Causal Body of God.

Since the dawn of the New Millennium, a very elaborate Divine Plan has been unfolding step-by-step involving the G-d Selves of all Humanity and the entire Company of Heaven. The plan has assisted in preparing Humanity for the moment when the Earth and all her life will be ready to receive the patterns of perfection from the Causal Body of G-d that will result in the tangible manifestation of Heaven on Earth.

With the incredible outpouring of love, compassion, generosity, friendship, unity and oneness that expanded through the Heart Flames of Americans and people throughout the world after the events of September 11th, Humanity reached the critical mass of preparedness. Now all is in readiness, and it is time to implement the next phase of the unfolding Divine Plan. The fulfillment of this phase of the Divine Plan will result in effectively expanding the Divine Intelligence within the Flame of Transfiguring Divine Love that is now pulsating in every person's Heart Flame. As that Divine Intelligence expands within every person's heart, it will push to the surface of the conscious mind, and expose in the Light of Truth, the distorted belief systems that are preventing people from remembering they are Beloved Children of G-d and that they are One with All Life. The acknowledgment of these Divine Truths is a critical factor that will awaken even the most depraved souls.

It is impossible to sustain the dog-eat-dog, worthless, worm-in-the-dust consciousness once people remember within the Divinity of their own hearts that they are Beloved Children of G-d and One with ALL Life.

The Legions of Light in the Realms of Illumined Truth have said that the assistance the victorious accomplishment of this phase of the Divine Plan will give to the recalcitrant souls who are in danger of not awakening in time to make the shift is beyond our comprehension. The Beings of Light are imploring every Lightworker to respond to the Clarion Call of our Father-Mother God. The Spiritual Hierarchy is beseeching us from the very core of their Beings to listen to the inner promptings of our G-d Selves. Every awakening Lightworker has been prepared to assist at some

248

level in the fulfillment of this vital phase of the Divine Plan. We are being asked to listen to our G-d Selves and to respond with courage, trust, willingness and confidence. We must not allow our manipulative human egos to prevent us from fulfilling our facet of this glorious Divine Plan with thoughts of lack, limitation, insecurity, failure consciousness, unworthiness or any of the other ploys our egos use to prevent us from accomplishing our Divine Missions.

After the opening of the Portal for the Causal Body of G-d which occurred in August 2000, the anchoring of the Flame of Transfiguring Divine Love in every Heart Flame which occurred in August 2001, and the opening of hearts that took place after September 11, the frequency of vibration on the planet has finally accelerated to a rate that will sustain the Matrix and Archetype for Divine Government. In order to fully understand the significance of that monumental feat, we must comprehend what Divine Government truly is. Divine Government First of all, Divine Government is not One World Government, a New World Order or any of the other concepts that have been used to describe the manipulative, controlling shadow governments ruled by the embodied forces of imbalance.

Divine Government is the antithesis of that level of consciousness. Divine Government is a perceptible manifestation of the Universal Law: As Above, So Below. It is a governing body comprised of the higher intelligence of the G-d Selves of all Humanity: a government of our Divine Selves, by our Divine Selves, for our Divine Selves. When we truly understand just what that means, we will begin to get a tiny glimpse of the colossal effect Divine Government will have on the world and all life evolving here. Our G-d Selves are the true expressions of who we really are as Beloved Sons and Daughters of God. The higher intelligence of our G-d Selves is what we have often referred to as our super-conscious mind. This aspect of our true G-d Reality is one with the Divine Heart and Mind of God.

Consequently, our G-d Selves clearly understand the Divine Principles governing this Earthly school of learning, and they know the urgent need of the hour. Our G-d Selves know that all life is interrelated and that if the Family of Humanity is going to survive, the human race has to come together as one unified force of Divine Love, Harmony and Balance. Our G-d Selves also know that every evolving soul is going through a unique learning experience on Earth and that our various races, religions, creeds, beliefs, cultures, nationalities and lifestyles are part of that learning experience. They know that, unfortunately, our human egos have manipulated us into creating gross mutations of the original Divine Intent of those learning experiences and that much of what we are expressing through our diversities is distorted at this time. When our G-d Selves have taken full dominion of our Earthly bodies, however, we will revel in the beauty and wonder of our uniqueness, and we will joyously honor each other as we share our differences. When our G-d Selves are governing our individual and collective lives, we will know that through our diversities we can learn and grow at a greatly accelerated pace. We will then graciously give our gifts, talents, wisdom, knowledge and abundance to enhance the lives of all people. We will understand that the G-d supply of all good things is limitless and that we are co-creating this reality together. Once the Matrix and Archetype for Divine Government are activated in the physical plane, the obsolete, fear-based cup of human consciousness will be shattered and the patterns of perfection in the Causal Body of G-d that are associated with Divine Government will be available to flow into the hearts and minds of every human being.

This miraculous event will greatly expand the Divine Intelligence within the Flame of Transfiguring Divine Love through every Heart Flame. As even the most resistant souls begin to awaken, their G-d Selves will be able to take command of their thoughts, words, actions and feelings. Eventually each country will be governed by the G-d Selves of the people abiding in that country. Since our G-d Selves know the full significance of the oneness of all life, they know that only by working toward the highest good of all concerned in every facet of life will we succeed in accomplishing the Divine Plan. Only by creating win-win situations in every governmental exchange, every human exchange and every exchange with the environment and the nature kingdom will there be Eternal Peace and Limitless Abundance on Earth. When our G-d Selves are governing the planet, they will easily reach into the Causal Body of G-d and tap into the viable solutions for every problem manifesting on Earth. They will tap into the patterns of perfection governing the Universal Laws of Energy, Medicine, Health, Healing, Economy, Food Supply, Shelter, Technology, Communication, Travel, Education, Science, Sacred Geometry, Music, Art, Movement, Meditation, Spiritual Growth, Enlightenment, Eternal Peace and every other pattern of perfection.

I know that when we observe what is taking place in the world it seems as if it will be in the far distant future before Humanity's G-d Selves will finally be governing the planet, but nothing could be further from the Truth. Actually, there are literally millions of awakening Lightworkers who, at this very moment, listen and respond to the Divine Directives of their G-d Selves the majority of the time. In order for Divine Government to manifest on Earth, it does not mean that every single person on the planet must be guided full time by his or her G-d Self. It means that those who are elected into public office, those who are in charge of governments and justice systems and those who hold positions of authority, power, education, leadership, security, etc., in every country must be guided by their G-d Selves full time. People in those positions are obligated to model the principles of Divine Government for the rest of awakening Humanity with every thought, word, action and feeling they express. The next phase of the glorious Divine Plan is designed to activate the Matrix and Archetype for Divine Government into the physical plane which will bring into manifestation sooner than any of us would dare to dream the scenario I've just described. Implementing The Divine Plan Two years ago we were guided by the Spiritual Hierarchy to arrange to have the Sixteenth Annual World Congress On Illumination in Washington, DC, in August 2002. As is often the case, we did not understand the full magnitude of that request at the time. Every facet of the unfolding Divine Plan is contingent on how much is accomplished during the previous phase of the plan. Not even the Company of Heaven knows exactly how successful the Lightworkers will be with each activity of Light until it is completed. Only then is an evaluation made and the next phase of the plan determined, according to the greatest need of the hour. In this case, the Spiritual Hierarchy has indicated that the facets of the Divine Plan that have been accomplished since the dawn of the New Millennium have far exceeded even the greatest expectations of Heaven. As a result, the next phase of the plan will catapult Humanity and the Earth a quantum leap forward up the Spiral of Evolution.

The reason we were asked to organize the Sixteenth Annual World Congress On Illumination in Washington, DC, on August 17th to the 22nd, 2002, is because that location represents the heart of government for the most powerful country in the world. America represents the microcosm of the macrocosm for the planet. The original Divine Intent of this country was to model to the world the unified Family of Humanity. We were supposed to demonstrate Humanity living together in harmony, prosperity, equality, happiness with liberty, freedom and justice for all-One Nation under God. All of our sacred documents: the Declaration of Independence, the Constitution and the Bill of Rights proclaim that Divine Mission. In spite of the errors we have made as a country and the corruption that has been demonstrated in our government off and on since its inception, that original Divine Intent has not changed! AMERICA is an anagram for the I AM RACE. The New World was to be a blueprint of Divine Government for all the world to see.

The I Am Race was to be a race of God-Conscious souls comprised of every race, religion, culture, nationality, creed and lifestyle. Even though it seems we have fallen far from the original plan, the Blueprint for Divine Government is pulsating in the Spark of Divinity for this country, and it is now time for the Matrix and Archetype for Divine Government to be activated. Once the Matrix and Archetype are activated for any creation, the unformed Primal Light of the Universe is magnetized into the Matrix, and the Archetype begins to become a manifest form. That means, both literally and tangibly, that once the Matrix and Archetype for Divine Government are activated, nothing can prevent the manifestation of Divine Government on Earth.

In order to accomplish this miraculous activation, G-d NEEDS A BODY. For the Light of G-d to accomplish something in the physical plane, the Light must flow through the Divinity in the heart of someone abiding in the physical plane. It is not a coincidence that the events of September 11 have evoked unprecedented patriotism in the hearts of Americans at this crucial time. As Americans rekindle the joy, pride and love in their hearts for this country, the Light of G-d is flowing through their Heart Flames into Washington, DC. That activity of Light is preparing a powerful forcefield of Unmanifest Divine Potential. That forcefield will greatly assist with the fulfillment of the phase of the Divine Plan we are now being called upon to help with by our Father-Mother G-d and the entire Company of Heaven.

The Spiritual Hierarchy has asked those of us at the New Age Study of Humanity's Purpose, Inc., to send forth a Clarion Call to Lightworkers all over the world to inspire them to come to Washington, DC, to serve as surrogates on behalf of Humanity and as Instruments of G-d in activating the Matrix and Archetype for Divine Government. Those of us gathered at the 16th Annual World Congress On Illumination in Washington, DC, will create a Chalice of Light through the unification of our Heart Flames. Together we will form a mighty transformer through which the Light of G-d will pour to activate the Matrix and Archetype for Divine Government in the physical world of form. The more Lightworkers who respond to their Heart's Call and come to the World Congress in Washington, DC, to serve as the Heart, Head and Hands of G-d on behalf of ALL Humanity, the more successful the activation will be.

Often our human egos manipulate us into believing that we are just one small soul out of billions. What difference can one person possibly make? Well, that illusion is designed to prevent us from trusting our G-d Selves and from fulfilling the part of the Divine Plan we have been preparing for aeons of time to accomplish.

In Truth, you are a magnificent, multifaceted, multidimensional reflection of our Father-Mother G-d. You are a radiant Sun expressing ALL of the various frequencies of Divinity pulsating in the Causal Body of G-d. You are a G-d or Goddess standing on the threshold of the greatest leap in consciousness ever experienced in any System of Worlds. One tiny Ray from the Sun that you are is projected into the physical realm to sustain a physical body for your Earthly learning experience. When you join together with other Lightworkers who have the Divine Intent of serving as surrogates on behalf of Humanity and as Instruments of G-d, your G-d Self takes full dominion of your Earthly vehicles and the full-gathered momentum of your Sun radiates through your Heart Flame to accomplish your unique facet of the Divine Plan.

The intensity of that Light is unfathomable. When the Light of your Sun blends with the Light of the Suns of the other Lightworkers who have gathered with you, it expands exponentially. Through the unified Heart Flames, the Light of a thousand Suns is projected into the physical plane of Earth to accomplish the Divine Plan and to assist in awakening the rest of Humanity.

Don't ever underestimate yourself. You are a wondrous Child of G-d, and ALL that our Father-Mother G-d has is yours. For those of you who do not feel the Heart Call to come to Washington, DC, to participate in the Sixteenth Annual World Congress On Illumination, know that you still have an important role to play in the fulfillment of this phase of the Divine Plan. Listen to your heart, and ask your G-d Self to reveal to you how you can be the most effective Instrument of G-d during this momentous event. Words cannot express what a sacred honor it is for me to be able to walk this sweet Earth with you. Thank you with all the love of my Being for volunteering to be on Earth during this incredible Cosmic Moment.

Thank you for remembering who you are and for fulfilling the purpose and reason you have come to Earth. The Company of Heaven stated that there has never been a moment in time when it was more imperative for us to fulfill our highest potential as Lightworkers. They have indicated there are several things we can do to increase our ability to be effective Instruments of G-d. We are continually being guided by these Beings of Light according to our individual Divine Plans…..

A final note….

I would like to express to each of you that these visions and synchronicities which have blessed my life are herein written to encourage you, the reader, to pay attention to your dreams, to follow your heart and intuition, but most importantly, to honour yourself. Seek like-minded people, and find your purpose, be the Lightworker you are meant to be, and God-Self participating in this New Golden Age.

The Goddess in me honours the Goddess in you. Namaste

…..*Rosaline Temple*

PART 2

The Swan Stargate

22:22 *"The Diamond Heart Activation"*

"After twelve years of longing to visit two very special places, my wish finally came true. In 1995, I began having many dreams and visions, in which I travelled "out of body" to Egypt and Jordan. These were life-changing experiences for me, and I became passionate about wanting to be there on the physical level. On September 14ᵗʰ, 2007, I finally stepped foot on Egyptian soil. It was the trip of a lifetime, an exciting and emotional journey, but what happened upon my return, was so profound, that I felt compelled to document and share this unique and extraordinary story.

"The Crystal Palace Meditation"

Find a comfortable spot in your home, a place that is private, but has a nice ambiance. Light a candle, burn some incense, put on some quiet music. You can sit, or you can just lie down, just get comfortable.

You may want to do a few stretches to begin with, and when you have settled down, you can begin by taking three deep breaths. Breath in through the nose, and out through the mouth. When you breath in, imagine yourself breathing in the feeling of love, and with each breath out, you are releasing all stress, all anger, all sadness and frustration.

You feel more and more relaxed, with each breath you take.

"Imagine that you are standing on a beach, gazing out towards the water. The sun is rising, and you can feel the warmth of the sun on your body. The sand feels soft and warm beneath your feet, and a gentle breeze is caressing your face and hair. Your clothing feels very loose and comfortable, and you are in a pure state of "being".

As you stand there, in your perfect state of relaxation, you notice a woman stepping out of the water, towards you. She is dressed in long flowing robes, and her hair is gently blowing in the breeze. With each step she takes, her clothing gently moves around her, and as she gets closer, you can't help but notice how "radiant" she is. The Goddess reaches out to give you a gift, and places it around your neck. As you look down, you realize that she has given you your personal mandala, your very own symbol, and it now rests gently on your chest.

She turns and begins walking along the edge of the water, beckoning you to follow her. In the distance, you can see a golden pyramid glowing in the sun. The goddess enters, and you follow. As you step through the entrance, you look up and see a name engraved on the archway above, and something inside you stirs – a memory. In the centre of the pyramid is a resting place, made especially for you. You take your seat, noticing how comfortable you feel. You call for protection from Archangel Michael, Archangel Metatron, and Lord Melchizadek. You ask them to accompany you, along with your "guardian angel". When you are ready, you call for your body of light.

Ever so gently, as the light descends upon your little pyramid, you feel the essence of pure love and the brilliant light shining through the top of the pyramid, encompassing you in celestial light. You feel yourself being lifted so carefully, high into the sky, and you ask to be taken to your island in the sea. You travel silently with the goddess, surrounded by the angels who protect you in your body of light. Eventually, from a distance, you see your beautiful island, surrounded in aquamarine water. The sand is the purest of white, and you can see palm trees, swaying in the breeze. In the very centre of the island there is a "crystal palace" sparkling like a diamond, and beckoning you to come.

Gently, the angels assist your little "pyramid of light" to land safely on the beach. The door magically opens, and you step out onto a beach. As you look towards the pristine water, dolphins swim up to greet you, and you begin walking in the sand. You can feel the warmth of the sun on your skin, and with each step you take, you can't help but notice how light you feel. There are crystals sparkling in the sand, and as you look ahead, you notice a pathway leading toward the centre of the island. White doves and butterflies accompany you, as you step onto this path, and the scent of roses permeates the air.

Eventually, you come upon a clearing of grass. At the far side, a white horse is grazing. He senses your arrival, and raises his head, allowing you see that he is not a horse, but the legendary unicorn. A garland of white roses surrounds his neck. Without a sound, he steps toward you, then gracefully lowers himself for you to climb on his back. He carries you off toward the crystal palace.

As you approach, you notice how it sparkles in the sunlight, and a sound so melodious and pure, beckons you to come closer. A golden band of light surrounds the palace, and you remember to put yourself into a state of "pure love" to pass through this golden ring. Upon entering the garden, the ground is covered in rose petals, the most beautiful shade of pink you have ever seen, its' perfume radiant, and envelopes your being. You stand there, breathing deeply, the colour permeates your being. You feel very connected to the earth, as if you were a very part of her. With each breath you exhale, the deep colour pink of the rose petals fills your aura.

Once inside the palace, you begin to climb the spirial stairway in the centre of the room. When you reach the first level, you enter a room filled with the colour orange. Beams of this orange coloured light emanate the room, and a beautiful fragrance permeates the air. A ray of this brilliant coloured light enters your body, and you breathe the intoxicating fragrance deeply into your being. As you exhale, this gorgeous colour fills your aura. As your eyes slowly adjust to the light, you notice someone standing in the centre of the room. They step toward you, placing their arms around you – filling you with a feeling of wholeness. In that moment, you realize that this is "that part of your self" that you have been searching for your whole life – your twin. You stand there feeling completely fulfilled, yet knowing that this is only a passing moment. Knowing that you will meet again when the time is right, you say goodbye and leave, ascending the crystal stair to the next level.

There, you find another room, this one surrounds you in brilliant golden light. A unique fragrance also accompanies this light. You allow the perfume to enter your body and as you breath out, your aura is filled with this radiant yellow light. Butterflies surround you, as you stand there, reminding you of the transformation that you are going through. They feel your love, and as you open your palm, one of them lands in your hand, and you sense the joy that the butterfly brings. You embrace the knowingness of change that is about to happen, and when your aura has absorbed all the golden rays, you ascend the stairway once again.

You hear a melodious sound. Two shimmering angels greet you – one is pure pink light, and the other, emerald green. Each of them take you by the hand and escort you into another room, and lead you toward several tall marble pillars. As you get closer, you can see that they stand guard over a large rectangular pool filled with pink coloured water. Your heart tingles, as you step into it, and your soul remembers how sacred this place is. Every atom and pore are restored to its original state of purity, and a healing takes place. Your being is filled with the feelings of forgiveness and gratitude.

When you ready, the angels lift you, carrying you to a much higher level. As they bid you farewell, you step inside another room. You notice a mysterious aqua coloured mist. Everything is very quiet, and you can gently see the sun going down through the large windows, and its rays appear to be gleaming and shimmering through this magical aqua dew. As you look down, you realize that there are several large golden discs, lying there, in front of you. Each engraved with a different symbol, representing love, happiness, good health, abundance and joy in every possible way. You are drawn to step upon those discs, and as you do, you feel the blessing of the golden symbols as they touch your soul. Further along, all by itself, you notice one more disc. As you approach it, you realize that this special disc represents your "gift of expression". However you wish to express yourself, to dance, sing, paint, or write –this disc can help to make your dream come true. You take one last step onto this disc, and you breath in the aqua mist, allowing it to permeate your being with its fragrance. And when you are ready, a door opens, and you you step through, onto a balcony.

It is night time now, and the sky is a beautiful dark shade of blue. The stars are twinkling like golden sparks of light, calling out to you, so gently against the velvet blue sky. As you stand there, a pure white eagle suddenly appears. You climb upon his back and he carries you into the mountains. When he lands, you notice that you standing near the top of a mountain. You are quite taken, and feel very serene. Eventually you look up, and notice The Goddess standing directly in front of you. She is dressed in pure white, and she appears magnificent, her radiance glowing against the beautiful midnight blue sky. The stars are twinkling like golden lights like you have never seen before. She takes you by the hand, and leads you into the darkness of the night. You smell the fragrance of roses once again, but you cannot tell where you are, but trustingly follow her. Eventually you hear the sound of water, and with each step that you take, the sound gets louder, until you find yourself standing directly beneath a waterfall.. As the water pours down upon you, purifying your being once again, you feel your heart opening, and your aura expanding. The sound of water slowly disappears, and you begin to hear the beautiful melody that called you to that place.

The darkness is gone, and you look around, realizing that you are now standing inside a beautiful temple. filled with amethyst coloured light. Violet rays are now permeating around you and throughout your being. You breathe in the colour, expanding the amethyst light into your aura. As you look around this temple, your eyes adjust to the light, and you realize that there are golden archways all around you, beautiful mosaic patterns of sacred geometry and beautiful writings in an ancient language are embossed on the walls, and there are windows of sparkling coloured glass mandalas. This is your temple, the one you created and where you can return to, whenever you feel the need.

You stand there quietly, enjoying the moment for as long as you wish, until you feel it is time to return home. The temple magically disappears, and you are surrounded by nature once again. You notice a small pond, with a white Swan swimming in the water. She invites you to climb upon her back, promising to take you back to the crystal palace. She gracefully floats along the water then ever so carefully takes flight. She returns you to the balcony. You step down and enter the crystal palce, and begin descending the crystal stairway. You pass by the room filled with aqua coloured mist, you say good bye to the pink and green angels, you pass by the butterflies, and your twin flame. You step into the rose garden, and pass through the golden ring of light, where the unicorn waits for you. He takes you back to the path that leads you to the beach, where the angels await with the Goddess. You step into your golen Pyramid of Light, and you call for your "light body" once again. You are lifted high into the sky once again, and with light speed, you return to the place where you began this journey. The angels and the Goddess bid you good bye. With palms together, you bring them up to your forehead, and say Namaste. When you are ready, you may open your eyes."

"Mystic" - *Rosaline Temple*

About the Author

It was through her dreams and visions that Rosaline Temple became interested in the wisdom of the ancient mystery schools of Egypt; and the sacred teachings of the Hebrew mystics, known as Kaballah. Realizing the profoundness of these divine revelations, she began integrating the visions and knowledge into her artwork and her teachings.

Her home is a "Rose Light Sanctuary" where she hosts meditation and workshops about "The Universal Flower Language" and "Twin Flames". She is also a certified Reiki Master, specializing in "Rose Reiki". Initiation" ceremonies for those drawn to the "Sisterhood of the Rose" are also held. As an "artist of the light" she is now offering her clients "Spiritual Essence Portraits" - a painting created specifically for them, based on their personal information.

Rosaline Temple lives in Enderby, British Columbia, Canada, with her husband. Her passion is to travel to sacred places, reconnecting with the energy and leylines of the Earth, and to share her "mystical experiences" with the world. For more information, please visit www.RosalineTemple.com

"Mystic" - Rosaline Temple

Bibliography

"Embraced by the Light" - Betty Jane Eadie

"Angels & Oranges" - Erin Caldwell

"The Seven Beloved Archangels Speak" - Thomas Printz

"The Crystal Stair – A Guide to Ascension" - Eric Klein

"The Celestine Prophecy" - James Redfield

"Kryon Book 2" - Lee Caroll

"The Keys of Enoch" - J. J. Hertak

"The Ancient Secret of the Flower of Life" - Drunvalo Melchizadek

"The Popol Vuh" - Francisco Ximenez

"Animal Speak" - Ted Andrews

"Mahatma I & II" - Brian Grattan

"The Camino: A Journey of the Spirit" - Shirley Maclean

"Permutation, A True UFO Story" - Shirle Kline-Carsh

"The Lords of the Seven Rays: Mirror of Consciousness" –

Mark. L. Prophet & Elizabeth Clare Prophet

"The Light Shall Set you Free" -

Norma J. Milanovich & Shirley D. McCune

"My Baba and I" - John Hislop

Bibliography

"The Woman's Book of Healing" - *Dianne Stein*

"The Mysteries of Isis: Her Worship and Magick" - *DeTraci Regula*

"Words of Power" - *Brian and Esther Crowley*

"Z-5, The Secret Teachings of the Golden Dawn - Pat Zalewski

"The Secret Doctrine of the Rosicrucian Order" - *Magus Incognito*

"The True and Invisible Rosicrucian Order" - *Paul Foster Case*

"Initiation in the Great Pyramid" - *Erlyne Chaney*

"The White Rose" - *Theodore Bromley*

"The Hiram Key" - *Robert Lomas and Christopher Knight*

"The Life and Teaching of the Masters of the Far East" - *Baird T. Spalding*

"The Emerald Tablets" - *M. Doreal*

"The Lineage of the Codes of Light" - *Jessie E. Ayani*

"The DaVinci Code" - *Dan Brown*

"Holy Blood Holy Grail" -

Michael Baigent, Richard Leigh, & Henry Lincoln

"The Orion Mystery" - *Robert Bauvall and Adrian Gilbert*

"The Zohar, the Book of Splendor: basic readings from the Kaballah" -

Gerhsom Gerhard Scholem

"Mystic" - Rosaline Temple

Made in the USA
Charleston, SC
15 February 2012